STIRRING THE POT

STIRRING THE POT

Always a good idea to keep things stirring. Traci

By Emmy Award–Winning Journalist
Traci Mitchell

NEW DEGREE PRESS

STIRRING THE POT

ISBN

978-1-63730-453-2 *Paperback*
978-1-63730-563-8 *Kindle Ebook*
978-1-63730-564-5 *Digital Ebook*

To every woman and girl,
you have the power to disrupt the universe.

Especially you, Peyton.

CONTENTS

———

ACKNOWLEDGMENTS

———

I want to thank my incredible mother. You were the first to stir the pot. I'm sure you're in heaven still stirring the pot. You are the strongest, most amazing woman to have ever walked in my world. Your grace, courage, and love live within me.

Thank you my Roy, for being my rock and my source of comfort. I love my life with you. My loves, Trey and Peyton, having a front seat to watch you grow up has been my greatest joy. Thank you for choosing me to be your mother. I love you. Tanya, you were my seatbelt back when we didn't have any. Thanks for still holding me close and always having my back. Laci and Dwayne, my other two children, I'm so proud of you. Daddy, thank you for continuing to stand strong. My family has always been my foundation. Thank you all for putting up with me through this process and every day of my life. I know it's not always easy.

My deepest gratitude to Eric Koester. I love your energy and your drive. My editing team, Paige, Leilani, and Linda, thank you for helping my words come alive and pushing me when I thought I would never finish. Thanks to Brian and the publishing team. I see you, Mackenzie and Kyra. Thanks to my marketing genius, Kelly Bedrossain.

My amazing friend Heidi: this is all your fault. Thank you for making this book possible. Lorelei and Marcy, you really pulled me through this. Thank you for reading the rough, rough draft.

A huge thank you to all my early supporters, my dearest friends. You believed in me long before I finished writing. I leaned on your support on my most difficult days. You inspire me. Thank you: Aleta C. Waters, Janet Crenshaw Smith, Tanya Darensburg, Desiree Brown, Susan Dozier, Richard Gervase, Erika Mobley, Lester Love, Gillean Smith, Marilyn Potts, Frances T. Watson, Kenneth Bazile, Madoline Bealer, Jaclynne White Nnawuchi, Faye Cobb, Kenyan McDuffie, Princess McDuffie, Lynda Keese, Eve Hill, Angela Bradley, Denise Wardlaw, Linda Simon, Amy Palumbo, Lorelei Cooney, Trish Yan, Desmond Dunham, Helen Hebert, Tamela Hebert, Ashli Clanton, Arvyce O. Walton, Orysia Stanchak, Janice S. Gin, Stepheny Luke-Andrews, De Etra Branch, Shawn Morgan, Sirwanda Hall, Margaret A. Gaylor, Vicki Breaux, Marion Alexis, Erin Aslan, Stephanie Reiners, Vicki Schultz, Tondra Vest, Nicole Barr, Shaute Thomas, Vanessa Reed, Brittany O'Grady, Nicole Corning, Heidi Junk, Jennifer Jones, Linda Beebe, Shanda Quintal, Dwayne Darensburg Jr., Mary Zitello, Christine Worrell, Tanya Hutchins, Angela Davis, Jasmine Browner, Eric Koester, Erin Lubin, Michael Carrier, Kimberly Young Matherne, Amy Smith, Rémie Christ, Lynette Mitzel, Richard Joseph Tancreto, Cynthia Schnedar, Lynda Williamson, Fred Hargrove, Mike Farber, Crystal Mack,

Mike Petruccelli, Valarie Ashley, Na-Rae Ohm Petro, Soyini Edwards, Marina Bowsher, Kathy McDonald, Tenikka Smith Hughes, Lauren Krasnodembski.

Thank you to all my wonderful friends who brightened my day or lightened my load while I was writing this book. It was hard! I so appreciate the words of encouragement, the calls, and the push I needed to get it done.

INTRODUCTION

—

The food, culture, and the people of New Orleans shaped my view of the world. As a child, I thought everyone had gumbo for dinner. They made groceries instead of buying them. And, when you met someone, you asked "ha ya momma n'em?" You didn't need a reason to have a party, and at every party, someone was always in the kitchen stirring the pot.

I don't remember how old I was when my parents started what became a weekly gathering. Every Friday night we would hear a knock on the door or the ringing of our doorbell. It was the kickoff to a party that never offered an invitation or an announcement. Everyone just knew they could show up at the Mitchell house and stay long past midnight. Sometimes when we woke up in the morning they would still be there— drunk and asleep, but still there.

Even as young children, my sister and I mingled with the guests or stood still long enough to hear a story that was usually too raw for innocent ears. From time to time, my dad would let me and my sister bartend. Yes, at a very early age, I learned to mix a pretty solid cocktail. Popping a top on a bottle of beer was easy. Making sure that the splash of Coke mixed perfectly with rum took precision. Drinks flowed freely, but it was the food that everyone eagerly awaited, especially if it was my mom's prized gumbo. She would literally cook that gumbo all day long, getting up every hour or so to stir the pot. Every time she stirred, I knew something good was coming.

Stirring the pot conjures up memories of days long gone, reminds me of the comforting presence of my mother, and sparks a fire that lights the way forward on my own mean-ingful journey.

Everything that makes us who we are comes from our memories, from our experiences, and from the people who come and go and touch us in a multitude of ways. It has to do with why we are here. I believe our lives are a part of a grander plan. You ever wonder why you're amazing at some things and terrible at others? Why some things bring you incredible joy, while others suck you down a dark hole? It's all part of a bigger plan.

Your gifts were put in place long before you stepped foot on this earth. God or, if you prefer, the universe has big dreams for you. You just have to embrace them and live your mission.

How do you do that? Lean on others who are living their purpose. You know them, the people who always seem joyful and fulfilled. They seem to have a constant pipeline of success. Their talents seem perfectly fit for them. They're like magnets. You just flow naturally towards them.

Entrepreneur Rachel McKenzie is one of those people. She did not know it then, but she started on the path to finding her purpose as young as twelve years old. Her young mind mastered hooch and wine making in her bedroom at night and figured out how to turn a profit. She now has dreams of being a billionaire. It isn't just money that drives her. Faith, family, and the need to make a difference are key.

I wondered if Rachel's journey was unique or part of a larger trend, and what I have found has changed the way I see how each of us should approach our journey to find meaning in life.

Study after study has shown that having a sense of purpose improves physical and mental health and the overall quality of life. It gives you a reason to get up every morning, keeps you connected to family and friends, and helps you sleep better at night. Purpose is linked to better cognitive functioning and greater longevity. Researchers believe people take better care of themselves when they have a reason to live. One study tracked thousands of people over fourteen years and found that the people with greater purpose were 15 percent less likely to die at a young age than the people who were aimless. Living with purpose can add years to your life. (Hill, Turin, 2014)

If you follow your talents, strengths, passions, and all the things that bring you joy, they will lead you down a path to find your purpose. Even those times of great pain and suffering are preparing you for your own greatness.

Each of us has our own gifts and talents. They're as unique to us as our dreams. We also have burdens and responsibilities, and we get weighed down with the heavy load. We're so busy taking care of everything and everyone else that we are less likely to make time for our own passions and purpose.

Self-care is becoming elusive. We are not putting ourselves first. We struggle with self-doubt and a battered self-esteem. Not all of us but many of us. We're constantly hearing messages like you're not strong enough, smart enough, or just simply not enough. Look good, but be quiet. Wear makeup but not too much makeup, or be thin but not too thin. The messages are mixed and, I think, pretty messed up.

Dr. DaCarla Albright stresses the importance of living your authentic self. She warns that if you don't love yourself and practice self-care, you allow others to take over your life. Unfortunately, she knows. She kept a deep, dark secret for years that nearly killed her.

As a journalist I have spent decades telling stories of tragedy and triumphs, listening to victims and victors, and meeting people who wore the armor of heroes and heroines—people who are making the impossible possible. I wanted to know how they were doing it, what made them special, and what they knew that the rest of the world didn't. You'll meet women like Rachel McKenzie and Dr. DaCarla Albright in the chapters of this book. They bare their souls and share secrets of their calling, their purpose. They have big dreams just like you. So, why are they following their dreams and reaching unimaginable heights and you're not? You'll find out.

Their stories stirred something in my soul and ignited a fire. They remind me of a moment that changed my own journey back in 2005. I was working as a Washington correspondent covering national news in Washington, DC. Oprah Winfrey would host the *Live Your Best Life Tour* with a stop in DC. Of course, I wanted to live my best life, but tickets to the event sold out before I could put my hands on one.

In one of my moments of dreaming really big, I decided I would personally ask Oprah and share what I learned. I made what seemed impossible possible. I reached out to everyone I knew, my boss, friends, magazine editors, the cousin of a someone who worked on Oprah's show—really, everybody. I really wanted to know how Oprah does it. How she lives her best life. After digging in for days, confirmation arrived. I was invited to the press line where I could ask Oprah one-on-one questions before the event started and sit in on the first few minutes of her onstage remarks.

When that day arrived, I watched her car slow to a stop just steps from where I stood. She got out of the SUV and waved at a large crowd of mostly women screaming and shouting her name, then she turned her attention and walked to the press line. When she stood in front of me, I knew my time was short, so it didn't take me long to get to the point. I said something like, "Oprah you are so amazing. Everything you touch seems to turn to gold. What is it about you that is so different and special?"

After hearing her words, I was—and continue to be—driven by what she said. I had been enjoying life but still living each day on repeat. I've learned to walk a different path, quieting my inner critic, and allowing a higher power to guide me.

I do occasionally lose my way, but here's what I know for sure: your purpose is always evolving and encompasses a wide swath of your life. At different stages, you may find purpose in the work you do or the time you give. Family and community may reveal meaning. You don't walk the path alone; along the way you will meet others, and connecting with them will provide even deeper meaning.

So, let's connect and hear the tales of women whose lives are so well woven that the unraveling of each delicate stitch reveals their vulnerabilities and their courage. Maybe some-where along the way you will feel that spark, that yearning that wakes up an energy that has always been there, giving you the fire you need to set out on your own meaningful journey. Maybe you will finally hear your inner voice and be guided by a higher power. Or maybe you will be inspired and uncover the courage you need to get unstuck.

Anything can happen, and it will. Dream, and when you do, dream big.

CHAPTER 1

YOUR SPARK

———

And so our mothers and grandmothers have, more often than not anonymously, handed on the creative spark, the seed of the flower they themselves never hoped to see—or like a sealed letter they could not plainly read.
—ALICE WALKER

I am not sure when I encountered it, but I definitely did. I found the light, the spark you feel deep down in your soul which convinces you that you can do anything. It makes your soul stir, your blood rush, and your heart beat faster. It makes you giddy. The joy is so incredible! That spark sends you on what you know is the right path. I have felt it many times in my life. My earliest memory of it happened in sixth grade.

On that day, our class was preparing for a speaker who would talk about their occupation and how incredible it was. We heard from doctors, lawyers, and government workers. It was usually someone's mom, dad, uncle, aunt, or grandparent. But this time was different. This time a news reporter came from the local news station.

I had never met a news reporter before—those people on TV who were not really real, most of whom did not look like me. And this woman didn't look like me either. She was older, probably in her thirties. I was around eleven years old, so thirty was old to me. She was also white. But what she said was so fascinating to me, I sat up a little straighter in my chair and was laser focused on her words. And I felt a spark. I had a clear vision. I knew my life's journey. I would become a news anchor. The fire was simmering deep down in my soul.

It was not an easy journey but I knew I would do it. I knew it so well I would stand in front of my full-length ivory-colored mirror every day and become that news reporter. I could see it happening right in front of me.

But, my reflection then is not how others saw me. My classmates told me my skin was too dark to be on TV. Some relatives told me the same thing and would remind me that I was an ugly baby. But it didn't matter that I was too Black, too ugly, or too loud according to other people's opinions. I knew the world would love me as much as I loved it, and I knew with every ounce of my being that I was destined to become a news reporter.

When I hit high school I took speech and typing classes hoping they would help. I was conditionally accepted into the Performing Arts School in New Orleans for singing and dancing. But I couldn't go to that school because I thought it would change my whole trajectory. So, why did I apply if I didn't want to go? Maybe it was because my friends and I watched a little too much of the TV show *Fame*. But while the thought of becoming a dancer was incredible, I knew deep down I wouldn't be happy until I was standing in front of that camera doing my part to change the world.

By my senior year in high school I was on my way. One of my classmates, Joya McGlory, left parting words, or quips as we called them, in my yearbook. She wrote, "Traci Mitchell, who is known by her full name, will grow up to be an anchorwoman but will still walk the same."

After college, I was considering three very different career opportunities. I could work for the IRS, Prudential, or a

TV station just outside of Boston. You know I chose the TV station. But first I had to beat out a long list of very qualified finalists who had applied for the same television fellowship at WCVB TV in Needham.

I flew into Boston early the morning of the interview and took a cab to the TV station in Needham. Shortly after arriving at the station, I realized it would be a crazy day of elimination. There were ten of us, including one of my very best friends, called one-by-one for the first round of interviews. If you made it, you were sent to the next waiting room. If you didn't, you had a premature arrival at the airport to board the next plane out. For the next few hours I went from waiting room to waiting room until it was down to only two of us.

The day had faded into night when I went in for the final interview. I sat at the end of a long boardroomstyle table facing a handful of people who worked at WCVB. They would decide my next steps.

They chose me. Or, should I say, I chose them because I had been walking this journey since I met the anchorwoman in sixth grade. I believed with all my being that I would win the fellowship and launch my long-anticipated career in TV news.

Quick sidebar ... as Joya predicted, Traci Mitchell grew up to be an anchorwoman, and I think I still walk the same.

I worked with the best of the best at WCVB for about one year. That's how long the fellowship lasted. After getting my chops, I got a job at WOWK TV in Huntington, West Virginia, where they let me anchor and gave me my own talk show.

Many times, I would be the only one in the studio. No floor director. No camera operator. Just me. I used Scotch tape to closely tape the news scripts together so I could get as many as possible on the teleprompter. Back then, the scripts rolled on a conveyer-style belt under the teleprompter. I ran my own teleprompter by pumping my foot on what I can only describe as a sewing machine pedal. When all the paper ran off the teleprompter and dropped down to the floor, I would call for a commercial break so I could jump out of my seat and lay more of those taped scripts on the belt. There was always a race back to my seat to beat the end of the commercial break. I did that dance for the entire show. It must have been hard to watch.

I moved from station to station and city to city landing at WGHP in High Point, North Carolina, then on to Cox Broadcasting in DC until I landed at one of the best stations ever—KTVU in Oakland, California. As one of the top markets in the nation, thankfully someone else was running the teleprompter. I was fortunate again to work with the best journalists in the business, and I still had that spark. I was on fire! I did amazing stories and had incredible opportunities. I even anchored with the great Dennis Richmond. But it was working with producer Leslie Donaldson that sent me reeling to new heights.

Leslie and I won an Emmy for our work on a story about the women of World War II. That Emmy reminds me of the wartime stories those fabulous, amazing, and hardworking women told. I became a journalist so that I could tell other people's stories and do my part to make a difference.

From KTVU I went on to cover the White House, Capitol Hill, and all things Washington, DC, for Hearst Television.

The urgency and the tight deadline pressure gave me a rush. The people, the places, and their stories made me dizzy with curiosity. I often wanted to know more. How did the story begin? How does it end? Where is she now?

I have always believed questions are the answer. How do we know what we don't know? Ask! There are people all around us doing impossible things every day, doing things we only dream of. As a journalist, I have had the incredible opportunity to continually feed my curiosity by asking questions. I've done hundreds of interviews and asked thousands of questions, maybe even more. One of my favorite interviews was with actor and author Henry Winkler. It's a favorite not because we got into a pillow fight in the television studio but because he's an all-around amazing person.

He walked into the studio alone. No paparazzi. No entourage. No driver. In fact, he took the Washington, DC, Metro. He said he was a little late because he wanted to swing by the Smithsonian to see his jacket—the leather jacket he wore in *Happy Days*. Could you imagine being one of the other visitors at the museum, checking out The Fonz's jacket, and looking over to see Henry Winkler himself standing there? I am sure he took many pictures, had many conversations, and gave tons of autographs, which is probably why he was late.

That was back in 2011 when I had left TV news and was the celebrity host for a lifestyle television show. As Henry Winkler and I sat down to get our mics on and get in position for the interview, I did what I do with every guest—I asked if he wanted to go over the questions. He quickly said no and explained that he is dyslexic and if he reads the questions it will throw him off.

I asked, "If you're dyslexic, how did you read the scripts for *Happy Days*?"

He told me he improvised or memorized. He didn't even know he had a learning disability until he was an adult.

Another fun fact: he doesn't actually know how to ride a motorcycle. Mindblowing!

We did talk about *Happy Days*, and he gave me the obligatory "Aaaaay!" catchphrase. But he was really there to talk about his mother's condition after her stroke. What I remember most was how Henry Winkler talked with such passion and from the heart. He really wanted to change lives.

Henry's dyslexia did not stop him from being a wildly success-ful author or from winning Best Actor awards. Later, during the CNN class of 2020 special, Henry Winkler talked about his academic struggles and the lessons he learned along the way. He says, "I was told I would never achieve. I'm in the bottom 3 percent academically in America. I took geometry for four years. Here's what I learned: none of that matters. What matters is you. What matters is what your gift is. What you're going to find inside yourself and you're going to give the world your power. That is the number one thing for you to remember." (CNN, Class of 2020 Special, 2020)

His message to students resonates with so many.

It took me decades of interviews—talking to the random person on the street, to leaders in the highest positions of gov-ernment—and an even longer time soulsearching to reignite my spark and figure out my superpower and what I want to give to the world.

I'm a storyteller. I'm telling the stories of others and my own story. I don't know what my next chapter will look like, but I'm excited to play it out. I believe we're all writing a book—the book of our own lives.

It's okay if the details of your life chapters are messy and rid-dled with mistakes. They're lessons. You learn from them and keep moving. You are capable of the impossible. Just believe it and lean on the gifts that are uniquely yours.

So my question for you is, what are your gifts? What is your superpower, your passion? How are you preparing for the next chapter? When are you going to give the world your power?

If you don't have the answers yet, you will be on a journey to find them by the time you finish this book. Here we go.

CHAPTER 2

OWN YOUR MAGIC

—

I realized that I don't have to be perfect. All
I have to do is show up and enjoy the messy,
imperfect, and beautiful journey of my life.
—*KERRY WASHINGTON*

In the late 1990s I was working in Washington, DC—covering all things political this time for Cox Broadcasting. I was invited to fly to Oakland, California, and give the keynote address at an event for Black Women Organized for Political Action (BWOPA).

I had been doing political live shots from DC for KTVU TV, which was owned by Cox in Oakland, as their Washington correspondent for several years. The morning anchors would toss to me, and I would give them report after report on the nation's news of the day. The people who tuned into KTVU for their news knew me. And even though I had done thousands of live shots and news stories, interviewed some of the biggest names in politics, and stood in front of that camera every day (sometimes even all day), I was a little nervous to give this speech.

I didn't know what to say. I didn't know how I would say it. I didn't understand why they wanted to hear from me. The invitation should not have been a surprise, but it was, and I wasn't sure I wanted to do it.

Full of doubt and extremely nervous, I agreed and started working on the speech. Draft after draft, it was still not ready. I wrote; I deleted. I researched; I deleted. I rewrote and rewrote again. When I was almost done, BWOPA called. They wanted to share the exciting news that Winnie Mandela would be speaking at the event. Yes, *the* Winnie Mandela—South African antiapartheid activist, politician, and ex-wife of Nelson Mandela.

My first thought was, "That's amazing!"

My second thought was, "Whew, I don't have to give this speech. I'm off the hook."

Wrong! Mrs. Mandela was only available to give a short speech right before mine at the event.

I paused—for a long, very long time. When I caught my breath, I said, "I'm sorry, but Winnie Mandela is giving a speech *before* me, and I'm *still* giving the keynote? Why don't I give a short speech introducing Mrs. Mandela, and she can give the keynote?"

I'm sure the woman explained why, but I stopped listening after she said it wouldn't work.

I was no longer focused on the speech. Finding a way to back out consumed my every thought. Winnie Mandela was the public face of Nelson Mandela during his decades of imprisonment. In the 1990s she had been tortured, banished, and banned and had risen to prominence. More doubt and fear creeped in as I knew I couldn't come close to that.

I went back to working on the speech knowing time was ticking. When the day came—I can't lie—I was still nervous. But I remembered what one of my mentors, Sarah Dunleavy, repeatedly told me when I was working my first news reporting job at WCVB TV in Needham: "Alert mind. Calm body." You may be freaking out inside, but on the outside stay calm and confident. No one needs to see you sweat. On that day no one saw any evidence that my nerves were rattled, not even Winnie Mandela.

Winnie Mandela presented an amazing, inspiring speech. The crowd gave a loud and long-standing ovation, but it still didn't drown my growing angst. How could I top that?

As I walked to the podium, crossing paths with Mrs. Mandela as she walked to her seat, she put her hands on my arms.

"You were amazing!" I spoke.

"You are, too," she said.

"How am I supposed to follow that?"

"Tell your own story," she replied. "You will be great."

Mindblowing!

I didn't need to top Winnie Mandela's speech. I just needed to tell my story and own it. I felt a crazy confidence in me as I delivered that speech—my speech, my story. At the end applause rang out. It wasn't as loud as what filled the room for Mrs. Mandela, but it was mine and I owned it.

We are often so busy trying to live someone else's story that we forget how to enjoy our own journey. Think about it: if your neighbor buys a new car, suddenly your car isn't adequate anymore, and you think about buying a new one. Your best friend gets engaged and you see her ring is bigger than yours, and now you need a bigger ring. We have all compared our status, achievements, material possessions, and even relationships to others, thinking if only we had what they had we would find fulfillment and success.

We all need to stop trying to walk someone else's journey. There is such beauty in enjoying your own ride and telling your unique story. Someone out there needs to hear your story.

Many years ago my husband and I were at the White House waiting for the taping of a PBS special, "In Performance at the White House: Women of Soul," hosted by President Obama and First Lady Michelle Obama. This was the mother of all events. It was the first time an "In Performance at the White House" would be all female vocals. The lineup included Aretha Franklin, Patti LaBelle, Jill Scott, Janelle Monáe, Ariana Grande, Melissa Etheridge, and Tessanne Chin. (In Performance at the White House: Women of Soul, 2014)

I'm not going to lie: I was super excited to hear Aretha Franklin and Patti LaBelle. Their songs are in my soul. They tell my story. It's the music I hear in the memories of my childhood. So, it was surreal to see Ms. Patti sitting right across from me.

But just when the action was about to kick off, I realized I needed to go to the ladies' room. If you have ever been to the White House, you know there is a process to getting in. It usually involves waiting in a long line, going through at least one security checkpoint, and walking down several long, Secret Service–lined hallways before finally making it to your destination. It takes a while, and there are usually no bathroom breaks.

I was on a mission to find a bathroom before the taping began. I was not going to make a scene in front of this crowd. So, I made an early beeline to the bathroom I passed on our way in.

As I was closing in on the ladies' room, I noticed a small posse of young guys hanging out. Now, remember, we're in President Obama's White House. Yes, there was music, but this was not a nightclub. It was odd to see a gathering outside of the bathroom.

When I walked through the bathroom door, I saw who they were waiting for: Ariana Grande. I know celebrities pee too, but it was weird seeing her in the bathroom. We were near the sink and mirrors, and she looked a little nervous. I expressed my excitement to see her perform. She confessed she was nervous and couldn't believe she was going to perform with Aretha Franklin and Patti LaBelle.

Oh, how I remembered being in her shoes!

I said something like, "You are amazing. You have your own talent and your own story. Aretha Franklin and Patti LaBelle are probably just as excited to hear you perform as you are to hear them."

Ariana Grande was incredibly kind and very thankful for my words. I'm not sure if my words made a difference, but she did seem more relieved, at least to me, as she left.

As I carefully walked in my way-too-high heels back up the long staircase to the room where the performance was about to kick off, I remember thinking, how crazy is it that this happened in the bathroom at the White House?

In his opening remarks President Obama told the audience to, "Hang on. The queen of soul is in the building. If she blows your mind, it's okay. That's what soul music does. It makes us move, and it makes us feel."

It was an incredible evening. The music definitely moved us, and the feeling was both electrifying and soul soothing.

One of the many memories that has stayed with me was right before Ariana Grande went on stage. Ms. Patti was holding Ariana Grande's hand and whispering in her ear. As she was called to perform, Ariana Grande thanked Ms. Patti and hugged her before walking up the stairs to center stage. She took a deep breath and belted Whitney Houston's "I Have Nothing." We may never know what was said between those two amazing women. Whatever it was, it was a prelude to an amazing performance and one more chapter in Ariana Grande owning her magic.

All the female performers rocked the house. Jill Scott, the boss she is, sang "Rocksteady" which is Aretha Franklin's song. How talented do you have to be to sing the queen of soul's song in her presence? That's who Jill Scott is!

In one of my favorite TED Talks, motivational speaker Caroline McHugh talks about the art of being yourself. She introduces her audience to Jill Scott and tells the story of a French filmmaker who is filming Jill Scott as she is about to go on stage following a performance of singer Erykah Badu. The filmmaker asks if she is nervous. (TED Talk, The Art of Being Yourself, 2016)

Jill Scott's response is priceless: "Have you ever seen me perform?" She goes on to say, "We all have our own thing. That's the magic. Everybody comes with their own sense of strength and their own queendom. Mine could never compare to hers, and hers could never compare to mine."

In that same TED Talk Caroline McHugh poses the question, "If you could be the woman of your dreams, who would you be?"

Think about it. Who would you be?

Starting today, stop trying to compare your queendom to others. Be the strong, fierce, and courageous woman you are.

Be your own dream. Start writing your next chapter of owning who you are. Remember, you're creating your own story, your own magic, and the world needs to hear it.

CHAPTER 3

WHO ARE YOU?

———

You have to love yourself. You have to prioritize yourself, and you have to stop putting yourself in a role. You have to live your authentic life.

—DACARLA ALBRIGHT

When my daughter was younger, she was obsessed with keeping her room clean. Everything had its place, and it was usually in a bag. Peyton had more bags than Whole Foods. They were tucked in corners, stashed under her bed, and lined in the closet. Every bag was loaded. We jokingly called her "the bag lady."

If you think about it, we're all bag ladies. Some we hide away, and others we try to carry. Sometimes the load is unbearable, even paralyzing. Yet instead of easing our load, we keep holding it and stay quiet about it.

A prominent lawyer in DC, a friend, finally divorced her husband. He had been abusing her shortly after they met in college. Even as a successful lawyer, she was stuck for decades under that unbearable load.

A dear cousin who was only eight years old was sexually assaulted by a boy at a house she and her family were visiting. When her mother called her to leave, the boy threw her off of him. She says he threw her like a piece of trash. When you're thrown like trash, it's hard to see your value. She carried that paralyzing bag for years. She finally unpacked it and pursued her purpose—helping others heal through their sexual assault trauma.

Women carry the weight of their own baggage and pick up the loads of others. We put everyone else ahead of our own passions and purpose.

At this moment, let's start unpacking our bags. Ask yourself who you really are. Think about it for a moment before you answer. I know, you're a daughter, sister, friend, employee, mother, or grandmother. But, if you strip away the labels, who are you deep down inside?

When I started writing this book I put out a call to my friends on Facebook asking if they knew anyone making the impossible possible, someone who was living her purpose. Several people suggested other women. The badass that she is, DaCarla Albright suggested herself. We scheduled a time to talk.

About a week later we were on the phone catching up. We had not spoken since those days back in the sacred halls of Ursuline Academy as schoolmates. We talked about old times and old friends and how Ursuline Academy gave us an outstanding education but didn't really feed our future selves.

Ursuline Academy is a predominantly white, all-girls Catholic school in New Orleans. It has a long history of educating girls and the distinction of being one of the oldest, if not the oldest, Catholic schools in the country. At Ursuline girls busily walked the halls in their crisp, white shirts and gray plaid skirts. Only a few girls looked like me and DaCarla. And there was only one Black teacher, Tina Doss—my favorite teacher. I know she looked out for the brown girls, but she never made it obvious.

DaCarla and I were not in the same grade, but we knew each other. All of the Black girls knew each other. DaCarla was a smart student and a loyal friend.

Even though DaCarla graduated at the top of her class, her high school counselor couldn't, or wouldn't, understand her dreams of becoming a doctor. She was told it might be a reach for her. But when you follow your dreams nothing anyone says or does can really get in your way. Your dreams are a part of who you are. DaCarla dreamed of being a doctor since sixth grade. And even though her school counselor didn't believe in her, her parents gave her the strength and courage to begin that journey.

DaCarla says, "I just have a lot of resilience. If there is a roadblock, I'm like, 'Yeah, okay,' and I may be upset about it for a day. Then I start figuring out how to get through it, under it, around it, or over it." She believes there is always a way somehow.

She dreamed well beyond the imagination of that little girl in sixth grade. Imagine how amazing our girls could be if their dreams were limitless and there was someone there to guide them. Where she stood, DaCarla was surrounded by men, mostly white men. She didn't have a guide and didn't know that it was even possible to dream the dream that would become her future.

She says, "I didn't have those people, or those mentors, in my life to know what else was possible."

She continued on her own path and made it through the challenges of medical school at the University of Michigan to become an obstetrician-gynecologist. She absolutely loved it but still felt like something was missing. She continued down the path of her dream and stepped into medical education at the University of Pennsylvania. She became the person medical students wanted to talk to, confide in, and ask for opinions. She says, "Through this resilience that I have, I was able to share tips and tricks from my own life. I've definitely had challenges. So, I was able to share with them and say, 'This is how you have to go through it.' It has now become my passion, and I started to follow that and see where it took me."

Stepping out of her comfort, she decided to apply for a dean's position at the University of Pennsylvania. Even though she had an amazing education, made it through the challenges of medical school, became a doctor, and was a badass about it, she thought she was only 50 percent qualified for the position. She struggled with her own doubt, as many of us do. But the people who chose her for the position, and quickly promoted her, knew she was 100 percent qualified.

DaCarla works hard and puts in long hours. She's smart and talented. But she understands not everything will work out; she won't win every battle or get every job she wants. She's human and has bad days, but that doesn't stop her from dreaming. She is always the optimist. When she does fail, she tries to find the lesson.

She says, "It's important for me to do my best and remain lifted to see the positive, to see the upside and the optimistic side, and to try to bring others along with me."

This is a lesson learned not just from living her passion, but from the trauma she faced in college.

As she was sharing all of the amazing things she was doing and all of the people she had helped, she was very clear that life is not always easy and that her life was riddled with its own challenges. "When I was a kid, my father said to me the first law of nature is self-preservation, and I didn't really understand what that meant until I needed to be quite self-preserving."

DaCarla was seventeen years old, and he was a year ahead of her. They met when she was checking out Washington University in St. Louis. When she started school there she contacted him. He was from her hometown, and he showered her with attention. She felt his comfort. He convinced her to move into his dorm. She didn't realize the attention was isolation. Just a few months into the relationship the abuse started.

As she had never seriously dated anyone, DaCarla was pretty naive and definitely in over her head. And, even worse, DaCarla modeled the actions of another girl, a senior, who stayed in an abusive relationship with her boyfriend even though he beat her up in public. DaCarla stayed with her boyfriend. No friends. No help. Just him. Their relationship waxed and waned. After the abuse there was always wonderful, romantic moments. It went on for years. Then, they got married. And the violent cycle continued.

When DaCarla started medical school, the abuse became cataclysmically bad. She was outpacing him, outgrowing him. She was in medical school, and he hadn't finished his degree. He was working a job and struggling. Even as she endured his abuse, she was crushing it. He was trying to hold her back.

"I know I had some toughness because I had a couple of good, good friends and classmates who would say, 'I would have failed out of medical school going through what you went through.' And I would say, 'Listen, my brain is all I have. And unless he kills me, he's not going to take my potential for this degree away. He's going to have to kill me.'"

And, he tried to kill her. "He put a gun to my head and played the equivalent of Russian roulette," DaCarla describes. "And once I survived that, I was like, 'You'll never get this chance again.' I was so terrified."

Terrified but tough, she became very calculating. She stashed money away and plotted to get out. She told people about her plans and finally told her parents about the abuse. Her biggest cheerleaders, her foundation of support, finally knew. Her wounds were open on full display. She was on a mission to get out. She found a domestic violence center and asked what she should do.

"I had to do this safely because this man tried to kill me," she says.

When he went out of town on a work trip, DaCarla moved her things and left a note. The university gave her privacy-protected student housing. They connected her with their student legal services, and she got a divorce for fewer than three-hundred dollars. She went through therapy and had the support of her family and really good friends.

It was years before she felt safe again. Even after all she went through, she says she doesn't have any hate in her heart for that person. "It's just sad that he had to do that to me and that his life was so harmed by other people that it was his pathology," DaCarla says.

DaCarla shares her story in hopes that it will help someone in some way. She even told her then fifteen-year-old daughter because she never wants her to walk a day in those shoes.

"You have to love yourself," DaCarla says. "You have to prioritize yourself, and you have to stop putting yourself in a role. You have to live your authentic self."

DaCarla doesn't let those seven years define her. But the lessons learned are valuable tools in her life and in her practice. She preaches self-care to new mothers and students, reminding them to take care of themselves.

"There is the mental, the physical, the emotional, the occupational. All these things are integrated in self-care. As women, we aren't validated in taking care of ourselves. We learn we should give away ourselves and we should be the last people to be given care. We learn this because we see our mothers do it. We learn that because we think that's great mothering. We learn that because we think that's what being a great wife looks like. Love yourself. If you don't love yourself, you negotiate your entire life away to other people."

Wise words from someone who lives them. As women, sometimes we are so locked into the cultural norm of being nurturers that we put ourselves last on our list of priorities, and everyone else's needs seem to come first. It is not selfish to take care of our own needs—such as getting enough exercise, eating right, and moving away from toxic people. When you discover your authentic self, no one can take that away from you.

So, I ask you again, who are you? And who do you want to be? Are you ready to unpack your bags?

CHAPTER 4

BELIEFS BECOME REALITY

—

It's not just in some; it's in everyone. And, as we let our own light shine, we unconsciously give other people permission to do the same.

—MARIANNE WILLIAMSON

It is amazing what we learn in kindergarten and how it shapes us into the adults we become.

My now nineteen-year-old son Trey was in kindergarten when his image of himself was rattled. I picked him up from school and immediately sensed something was off. Trey is the happiest child I know. Always wearing a smile, Trey is animated, is full of life, and talks nonstop. But on this particular day he was quiet, deep in thought. When my little one decided to speak he was clear and steady, as forceful as a five-year-old can be.

He said, "Momma, I'm Black. That means I have to work harder and be smarter than anybody else. Life is going to be harder for me."

That very second, my heart broke. I was sad, angry, and devastated. It's not something a five-year-old should know or believe.

I calmly asked, "Who told you that?"

Trey answered, "My reading buddy, Carter."

At Trey's school, the kindergartners had fourth grade buddies. They read together to strengthen their skills. And, apparently, they often went off topic. My first thought was, I'm going to chat with that little Carter. My second, more reasonable thought was to comfort my son and listen to his understanding of what he heard.

Trey and I talked for a while about his conversation with Carter that evening. The next day, as we were arriving at school, I asked Trey to point out Carter. I was definitely going to chat with his mother.

Trey literally pointed out Carter. Well, guess what? Carter is a girl. And, she's Black. It made me pause. All night as I thought about it, I was sure Carter was a boy and that he was any race other than African American.

Looking back, Trey says he doesn't remember the conversation with Carter, and it didn't change his beliefs. Whew! He added, "I was too little to remember that."

I bumped into Carter. She's in her twenties now. I asked if she remembered. She did. She says her mother always gave her that advice, and she felt she needed to tell my Trey. She thought she was sharing wisdom.

But little comments here and there do affect and change what we believe and how we see ourselves.

Have you ever walked past a mirror and taken a second look thinking the reflection didn't look like you? Or have you looked at a picture of yourself and thought there's something wrong with the camera? Maybe it's because we've morphed into other people's images and opinions of who we should be. Sometimes things that happen to us shift our beliefs.

I remember doing a story when I was working in North Carolina. A little girl had been shot by a boy in the neighborhood. They were both younger than twelve years old. Her neighbor had found and was playing with his dad's or brother's gun. When he went outside and started aiming it at kids in the neighborhood, they all scattered. As the little girl was running up her stairs a bullet hit her in the leg.

I was sent to the house to talk with her parents. I had already pictured in my mind that everyone in the house would be crying and in utter shock. They weren't.

When the grandmother, who was in her forties, opened the door, she was concerned but calm, not very emotional. We talked about what happened and how her granddaughter was doing.

I said something like, "This is so horrible, a child being shot."

She replied, "You've never been shot?" She went on to explain that everyone in her family had been shot at least once.

Now, I was stunned. No, I've never been shot, and no one in my family had either.

It was a reminder for me that beliefs become reality. In that family being shot was not shocking. It was almost expected, sort of like a rite of passage.

Understand the power your beliefs, your thoughts, and your actions have. Change what you believe, and it will change your life.

When we're little, our parents tell us who we are and what we should be. Then the voices of teachers, professors, friends, and significant others as we grow older take precedence. Boyfriends, husbands, and partners dig in too. Slow down. Take a minute and think about it. Who are you really? Who do you want to be? What are you doing with your life? Are you chasing someone else's dreams?

Lauren Krasnodembski, an attorney and creator of the Mind Muscle Motivator, says it's not just society that controls our thoughts and self-image. Major life events shake up your reality and turn things around—sometimes upside down.

Privileged and sheltered is how Lauren describes her childhood. Her dad was a very successful doctor, and her family didn't have a care in the world. She says her life quickly changed, "And then all of a sudden, flip the switch. My dad has a brain tumor and is supposed to die on the operating table. That showed me you have to be prepared. And so, at ten years old, I became like a fucking control freak."

Lauren's dad survived, but the close call was enough to unhinge the ten-year-old's world. Normal wasn't normal anymore. Fear consumed what was once a carefree childhood. It changed how she thought and how she lived. She had to be prepared and self-sufficient. She focused on working hard and getting a really good job.

Work hard she did, and she became an attorney but not because she loved it. She believed it was something that she had to do. "I did ask myself that question, like, why, why am I doing this? That's when I realized and made the connection early on in my childhood that holy shit, I'm doing this out of fear. Fear that I'm never going to have enough money. Fear that I'm not going to be able to take care of myself or my family. Fear that I'm going to let somebody down. It was all based on fear, every single thing that I was doing."

Her journey of looking within was long and difficult. It definitely was not done in a day. The more introspection she did, the more responsibility she took on. She then had her own family, and was working a sixtytoseventyhour work week as an attorney and as a caretaker for her dad after her parents' divorce. She added more and more responsibilities until she nearly broke.

"I started taking inventory of my own internal thoughts and beliefs about myself," she says. "And I literally tracked those thoughts and beliefs for thirty days straight, when I was able to see patterns in my life. And then I started to address those patterns of anxiousness, of not being enough, and overworking to overcompensate for the fear of not being enough."

You would never believe this bold, outspoken woman was once controlled by fear. It takes daily affirmations and constant practice. She's not always perfect, but at least she's conscious of it.

She says, "It took so much digging to figure out what my beliefs were, which ones were limiting, and what I actually wanted out of my life, and then mirroring my actions. Because again, mirroring the actions goes somewhat against societal norms to be like, 'Yeah at five o'clock I'm fucking done. I don't care if I'm salaried.'"

Lauren thinks most people, especially women, let life run them instead of running their own lives. One of the first steps in understanding your passions and purpose is changing how you see yourself, changing what you believe about yourself. If you can see yourself where you want to be or who you want to be, that can take you further than you can ever imagine. If you can't see it, you can't live it.

It really is simple, but, like anything else, it may take time and a little discipline.

Lauren is finally on the path of living her purpose and has created the Mind Muscle Motivator to help women find their missing link, change their beliefs, and do so much more. She says it's okay if you're still trying to get there. Her advice: "You don't have to figure it out. It's going to find you. Once you start taking aligned action with your actual desires, the universe is going to respond, and it will find you. That's how my passion found me."

Beliefs are so powerful. What you believe becomes your reality. Change your beliefs and you will change your life.

So, how do you start to change your beliefs? Start with changing your habits. For example, if you want to be more productive, wake up earlier. It's amazing how many things you can accomplish if you have more time in the day. You'll begin to see yourself as more productive. If you want to be more organized, pick a simple task, like making your bed, and do it every morning. Over time you'll want to tidy up the rest of the room, and you'll see yourself as an organizer.

You don't have to have it all figured out. You just need to believe you can figure it out and make it happen. It will take time, so give yourself the same grace you give everyone else. Learn to quiet your own critic and be patient with yourself. There's no road map, no secret sauce, and no right or wrong. It will take some digging, but you'll get there. And when you do the universe will respond. It's an exercise that should give you a clearer picture of why you're here on this earth.

If you believe you can't do it, you can't. But what if you believe you can? What if you take a baby step today to change your habits to change your beliefs? Imagine the possibilities.

CHAPTER 5

ARE YOU ON THE RIGHT PATH?

———

*It's a matter of embracing what's in front
of you and making the most of it.*

—HEIDI JUNK

Life has a way of throwing fastballs that you never see coming.
Sometimes you turn just in time to catch them. Other times
they knock you off your feet. We've all been knocked down.
We usually get right back up, but it is not always easy.

Luckily, we're not dodging balls every day. We are simply
living, we are always changing, and we are always on multiple
paths. No matter what path you are currently on or which
direction you are heading, make an effort to leave the place
you're at better than it was before you arrived.

That is Heidi Junk's passion. She strives to leave the place and
the people better than she found them.

Heidi and I met at the Cox News Bureau in Washington,
DC. She was a producer and I was a correspondent. Heidi
was smart, was full of energy, and had a great laugh. We
became fast friends, the kind of friends who shared stories
that others wouldn't understand and who always looked for
ways to lift each other up.

Heidi and I used to joke that we were somehow related because
we always had the weirdest ailments. We actually started
one-upping each other when it came to being sick. Once, I
developed a horrible sinus infection. It was so bad I lost my
voice for several days and struggled to get out of bed. My
doctor suggested surgery. I turned to a homeopathic doctor

who helped me discover that black fungus was growing on the plant that sat right next to my bed. I threw out the plant, and I was better the next day. I won! At least, I thought I did. Heidi had somehow developed something akin to bubonic plague (not really), and she won. I admit it was kind of a dark game, but it was a good feeling knowing you had a partner in a tough fight.

When I sat down to talk with Heidi about her purpose, she was same old Heidi—energetic, joyful, and excited to talk about the future. I asked her, "When did you feel like you were on the right path, heading in the right direction of your life?"

"That's a tough one," she said. "It's a matter of embracing what's in front of you and the opportunities that exist before you and making the most of them—and then waiting for the next track or path to become available."

Heidi knows about changing paths even when it is not your choice. As Heidi looks back over her life and career, she says her first path was in TV news. She loved the rush, the adrenaline of the business. At Cox she climbed the ladder from producer to the top job, bureau chief. She loved her team, and her team loved her back. Being in the trenches with others gave her energy. She was living her purpose, but life forced her to change directions as she tethered between a job she loved and a disease that was ravaging her body.

"For me that was being diagnosed with sarcoidosis." She says, "After two years of trying to continue on in a very demanding job which I absolutely loved, I realized that I could no longer do both, that I could no longer manage my disease and take care of myself."

Sarcoidosis is a rare inflammatory disease that forms tiny lumps called granulomas throughout the body. They can form in any organ but commonly affect the lungs and lymph nodes. The chronic inflammation can lead to scarring and organ damage or failure. For example, if they're in the lungs you may have trouble breathing. If the granulomas impact your central nervous system you might have nerve pain and weakness or numbness of an arm, leg, or part of the face. It has limited treatment options, and there is no known cure.

The disease forced Heidi to regroup and redefine while deploying a full medical team to manage the disease. She took time to really focus on what was right for her, asking herself, "What do I need, and what do I want? What I needed was to be able to have time for self-care and to be able to allow my body to heal—to really have time for physical and mental healing. And, what I wanted was to still be able to be fulfilled and still be able to feel like I was contributing and a value to society."

Sometimes taking a pause to do a personal assessment is exactly what we need. We must stop paying attention to everyone else and wanting what someone else has. Instead, you can do a deep internal dive to figure out what is right for you. What is it that you love? What makes you feel good about yourself? It doesn't have to be one thing. We are all multitalented. So, go ahead, start stirring your pot to see what you cook up.

Heidi figured out what she loved about her job, what it was that kept a smile on her face as she worked every day: she loved partnering with people. She loved talking with her team about their goals and their dreams. She would ask where they wanted to be in two, five, or ten years. She found joy in helping them to be the best they could be and achieve new heights.

"So," she says, "a spark ignited. Maybe there was something else out there that actually captures what I really love and what's really meaningful to me."

She found fulfilment in leadership coaching. Having had great value in coaching herself, she found it to be a natural next path.

Heidi says, "When we talk about a path, it's what is at my core. It's where my values are. It's what I love. It's what gives me energy, and it's a guide—like the gut. It's the thread that has been woven through all of these different aspects of my life."

Heidi finds it extremely meaningful to partner with people and help them meet the change they're seeking. Deep relationships with family and friends are important to her, as is the work she is doing with sarcoidosis research.

"I feel like we each have something we can give. We each have something we can contribute. We can all be looking at how we could lift each other up. How powerful would that be? There's something so important about us being there for each other. We see each other, hear each other, and feel that connectedness."

We do not walk this earth or in our purpose alone. Along the way we find others to lean on for support and knowledge and as cheerleaders to build us up mentally and emotionally. Even as Heidi continues to suffer from the effects of sarcoidosis, she doesn't let it define her or derail her purposeful path.

Always the coach and always looking for ways to help others, Heidi concludes with this: "It's important to create an awareness of what makes you happy and really gives you energy. You should also look into what might be holding you back."

Heidi believes your core values are key to living a happy life. They dictate your behavior and your actions. They drive your decisions and guide you even when you don't realize it. They determine what's important and meaningful to us.

If you are aware of them, you can be more intentional about how you're living and be more focused on inserting your values in your day-to-day activities. Knowing your core values helps you make better decisions and better choices. Living into them brings you fulfillment and joy.

Heidi shared this simple exercise: Think about a happy moment that you would never forget or a time when you were overjoyed, energized, or in your flow. What were you feeling? What was important to you at that moment? What values were being expressed? Select five of those core values and write a sentence about what each of them means to you.

Be completely open and don't judge your own thoughts.

I keep my core values on sticky notes on my desk to remind me of the values that are present when I'm in my flow, when I'm feeling on top of the world. They remind me of who I am when I'm at my best.

CHAPTER 6

HIGH DRAMA

—

What would happen if we were all brave enough to believe in our own ability? I think the world would change.

—REESE WITHERSPOON

When I sat to talk to Brittany O'Grady, I felt like I was meeting her for the first time. She was poised but kind, focused but funny, and far more mature than I had remembered. I knew Brittany long before she made her mark on the world. Her mother, Monique, is one of my oldest and dearest friends. In addition to a fabulous friendship, Monique has given me a front-row seat to watch Brittany grow into her purpose on purpose and be true to herself. It has been priceless.

Many moons ago, somewhere between college and various moves, I found myself temporarily taking up residence in one of Monique's bedrooms. She didn't charge me rent. I didn't charge her for babysitting. Besides, her girls were fun and easy. It was a joy.

After I had moved out, I stopped by Monique's house to introduce my new boyfriend—now husband—to the family. Monique opened the door with little two-year-old Brittany standing at her leg. Just as Roy and I were about to cross the threshold into her home, Brittany squatted like a professional athlete, reached under her dress as if preparing to hike a football, ripped off her diaper and flung it into Roy's arms. She giggled just as he caught it. Roy and I thought it was funny too. Her mom was mortified.

It wasn't the last time little Brittany surprised her mother. When Roy and I were planning our wedding we thought

Brittany's sister, Caitlin, would be the perfect flower girl to march down the aisle with my little nephew, Dwyane. They were the same age and really enjoyed each other's company. When Brittany found out, she lost it. She was just shy of four years old, but she knew what she wanted: she wanted to walk down that aisle as a flower girl. You could see her wheels turning. She batted her big, beautiful eyes and gave an award-winning smile. She made it clear that she should be the flower girl.

Our special day was Brittany's nightmare. She turned her head and pouted when her sister walked down the aisle. It was both sad and precious. So much so, our photographer captured that moment and all those emotions in her sweet little face.

Today, Brittany and I laugh at the memory. Unfortunately, she doesn't remember the details, but everyone tells her the story, and we have the picture to prove it. I half-jokingly told her she always takes it to a different level—just plain, high drama. But, hey, that drama and those intense emotions are part of what makes her Brittany. She thinks so too: "I have found my place. But it took a lot of time to find it and to find the strength in that." As a child, she says, "I did feel crippled by my drama and my emotions because they were so intense, and I had no idea why."

Brittany has been acting and singing for most of her life. She landed her first major television role as Simone Davis in the series *Star*. It was a tough job, a boot camp for the then nineteen-year-old. But she's grateful for it every day. The experience prepared her for what was to come. She says, "I would have never been able to do *Little Voice*. I wouldn't have survived it. I wouldn't have been able to create the character or have the discipline to not just say the words but learn the music and learn the choreography. I feel ready to work all the time."

Brittany's character, Bess, on the Apple TV+ series *Little Voice* is an emerging singer–songwriter. It's been her favorite job so far.

"I put a lot of emotional capital and dedication into that character," she says. "I felt the character was really near and dear to me, along with the woman who created her, Jesse Nelson. It was the best relationship I ever had with a creator. Jesse Nelson is just a wonderful woman. I felt heard. We understood each other. I felt creatively taken care of and a sense that she trusted me to do my job. I felt like we were set up to create a work that actually touched people on a soul level."

I don't know the entertainment industry as well as Brittany does, but I do know it's a lot of work. Brittany compares the process she goes through to get into character to much like how we live our lives every day. We can't plan every second, but we have to be prepared for anything. And sometimes we must live in the moment.

"It's kind of more intuition. I try not to overthink it too much because it distracts me a little bit." She adds, to get to know her character she sometimes creates a mood board or even a playlist. "It just depends. It's more of an internal process. Usually, the costumes help immensely because I'm physically wearing what the character wears, how the character expresses themselves, along with figuring out the words or the emotions of the character. Music helps too."

Brittany works really, really hard to touch people and she truly believes in her characters. She shows up with an open mind and is always listening to improve. She doesn't always know what's next, and that's okay.

"I think always being authentic and true to myself has led me to feel like I am living my purpose, whether it was acting or something else. I really do find authentic joy in doing the work and being able to tell stories and meet people."

Brittany is in her twenties, and she realizes that many people her age are still searching for their purpose. She recognizes how fortunate she is. "I'm blessed to be doing what I do, and if I'm meant to tell the story, it will be meant for me. It's just more about having faith in something bigger than yourself."

She believes purpose finds you when you're being true to yourself, despite what's happening around you and to you. Focus on faith, hard work, and perseverance. Whatever you choose or whatever chooses you, make sure you're in it for the right reasons.

Brittany admits that it's sometimes hard to stay focused, especially for actors who are constantly being judged and criticized. The darkness of self-doubt can be damning.

She says, "Most of the difficulty with pursuing my purpose is more of what happens in the industry—the inconsistency, working with people who can be bullies—but I think everybody experiences that in different forms at work. It can be difficult because you feel like you're a salmon swimming upstream instead of following what everybody else does to become successful. I'm not willing to sacrifice my morals."

Because she's a sensitive person, Brittany definitely absorbs other people's emotions. Over the years she's learned to set boundaries and has kept her circle of trust small. She talks to her mom every day and gets advice from her older sister. She also keeps her life balanced by exercising, cooking, and eating healthy.

Her advice is to find people who genuinely love you for you, and only allow those you trust in your corner.

Brittany has been brave enough to believe in her own ability both on and off the screen. She's incredibly talented but pretty self-effacing. I guess the quote by Steven Bartlett is true: "The most convincing sign that someone is truly living their best life is their lack of desire to show the world that they're living their best life."

You don't need an audience to live your best life. Be your own audience. Do it for yourself.

Your emotions and sensitivities are not disadvantages. They're your superpowers. They're a part of who you are. Find the strength and value in them, leaning on them in your career and everyday life. And, above all else, be brave enough to believe in your own ability.

CHAPTER 7

FOR LOVE OR MONEY

—

No person has the right to rain on your dreams.
—MARIAN WRIGHT EDELMAN

The Hearst Washington, DC, bureau capped off my long career in TV news. Here, we covered major news events for more than thirty television stations including the Hearst flagship Boston station, WCVB, which is where I got my first break. Hearst was my beginning and my end and where I had the most amazing boss, Peter Barnes.

During my first year at the bureau, Peter pulled me into his office and asked where I wanted to be in five years and how could he help me get there. I had already given it a lot of thought, and I was ready with my answer. I wanted to anchor a newscast.

Here's the problem: the bureau did not produce newscasts. Peter called the news director at our closest station, WBAL in Baltimore, and somehow arranged for me to be the weekend fill-in anchor. I was thrilled and a bit nervous because anchoring was not exactly my thing. I had not done it in years, and it's not like riding a bike. I beat down the nerves and walked into the WBAL newsroom like I knew what I was doing (like the saying goes, fake it until you make it). I made it through the first of many shows that day. My co-anchor, Lisa Robinson, and producer, Eliza Bulley, made it easy.

As one of three Washington correspondents for Hearst Television, I worked the day shift at first. Later, I switched to early morning so I could actually see Trey, my baby boy. I worked from two o'clock in the morning to ten o'clock, doing dozens of live shots every day before heading home to nap with Trey. Sometimes Roy would drop Trey off at the station in the morning, and Trey would spend hours playing at my feet on the floor while I did my last live shots. My photographer, Jeremy, would scoop him up just before he cried and run to the soundproof recording studio. It was brutal, but I wouldn't trade the time I spent with my son for all the sleep in the world.

Between anchoring at WBAL and covering all things Washington, DC, you would think I would be giddy. I wasn't. My coworkers were great. They were like family. Although Peter had gone on to another job, the new bureau chief Wendy Wilk was great too. Still, something was off. Working the morning, really overnight, shift had worn me down. Dogtired can't even come close to accurately describing how exhausted I felt. The reason I was working those crazy hours was so I could spend time with my family. But I was so tired that life was happening without me. I felt like a walking zombie.

A few years into those crazy morning hours, my daughter Peyton was born. I was on maternity leave for several months. Some of them I took without pay. I wanted to spend every moment with my little Peyton. Time seemed to fly. I knew I would be heading back to work soon.

We decided we would hire a nanny. Trey's wonderful nanny had already picked up two other families and wasn't available. We interviewed several people but couldn't find a good match for our family. We were excited when we received a recommendation from a friend. Her nanny had been with her a while and was ready to move to another family. We interviewed her, and she seemed great. We called five of the families she had previously worked for and they all gave stellar recommendations.

We hired her. She started a week before I went back to work. I was able to see her interact with Peyton and spend time with them throughout the day. When it was time to head into the office, I felt comfortable leaving Peyton in her care.

One morning, just two weeks after I returned to the studio, I had a break between live shots and decided to check my email. There were several from people on my neighborhood listserv. One email stood out. The subject line was, "Witnessed—Nanny abusing baby girl." My hands trembled as I touched the keyboard to open the message.

The writer said, "The baby girl is dark skinned with curly black hair and might be of Ethiopian, Indian, or African American origin. We witnessed the nanny roughly handling the baby girl on two occasions. Within a matter of minutes, I saw her violently shake the baby girl by her jaw and force a pacifier into her mouth. At first, I couldn't believe what I had seen, and it took a few seconds to register in my mind. When, again, the child continued to cry, the nanny forcibly grabbed the child by her jaw and lifted her by her jaw out of her stroller and onto her lap. She proceeded to look around her to see if anyone had witnessed her cruel actions, and when she felt she had gone unobserved, she roughly forced the pacifier back into the baby girl's mouth."

The email went on, "As a mother of two little boys, I was totally horrified and on the verge of tears. I felt compelled to do something to aid this baby girl. I went out to the nanny on the bench and confronted her and told her I had witnessed her behavior. She denied doing anything. I told her that both my mother and I had seen her. I warned her that if she did anything like that again to this baby, someone else would see her too, and she would not be able to deny it. I told her it was an evil act, reminding her that a mother had trusted her with the well-being of her child and that she was abusing the child."

The woman who wrote the email said she intentionally made a scene, and people started to gather. But, instead of questioning the nanny, they attacked her.

She added, "I felt really distressed to leave this defenseless child with this woman. I can only pray that I scared her so she will think twice about harming the child publicly again. However, I wonder how she treats the baby girl when home alone. I have also placed my children in the care of others whom I trusted. I have never been aware of my child being abused, but if they had been I would hope someone would somehow notify me."

I fought back the tears and calmed my nerves. With grace under fire, I immediately called my husband, who just happened to be home, and asked him to take a picture of Peyton with the nanny. I told him I had just read an email from someone who described our child being abused by a nanny. I ended our call.

When I received the photo I immediately sent it the writer of the email, asking her if the child and nanny in the picture were the people she saw. It was the longest few minutes I have ever waited. My heart pounded. My head hurt. I couldn't think or move. I opened the email the second it popped into my inbox. IT WAS MY BABY.

I was too hurt to cry and too furious to think.

I asked her to meet me at my house. I arrived just as she did.

Roy was on the porch protectively holding Peyton. He asked the nanny to come outside on the porch. It was clear that she was guilty the moment she saw me and the person who wrote the email. They got into a heated exchange, but nothing mattered at that point. Our child had been abused.

Roy had already packed up the few things the nanny had in our house. We gave them to her and asked her to leave.

We took our daughter to every medical specialist we could think of to see if there were any injuries. The doctors didn't find anything but asked us to keep a close eye on her over the next several days.

I stayed with her every second, hugging and kissing her, trying to love away the abuse. I wanted to erase away the pain that I couldn't protect her from.

We also talked to the police. They spoke with the nanny but couldn't, at the time, file charges because the witness said she would not testify in court. She didn't want to drag her own family through the process.

We understood and fully respected her wishes. Not everyone is courageous enough to speak up when they see something wrong. This woman may have saved our baby's life, and I will be grateful until I die.

I did go back to work. I went back to quit my job. I had been a journalist for almost two decades. I decided to leave it all behind because I chose love over money.

Here's what I quickly realized: your job does not define who you are. It's simply what you do. When I was no longer a news anchor, I was still Traci. When people no longer called me a journalist, I was still Traci. And being just Traci is beyond being good enough.

Besides, I was in full-on protective mode for both Peyton and Trey. After leaving my job as anchor and correspondent I looked for jobs that would give me flexibility. If I couldn't be with the kids, Roy was. When we had to travel, my mom would fly in to help.

I started working with several production companies and traveling around the nation. One day I would be on stage talking to an audience of eight thousand people. Another day I would be in the studio interviewing doctors about a new medication or a different use for one already on the market. I had a few other steady gigs, like celebrity host for a lifestyle TV show. It was new and different, not as fast paced as a newsroom, but I loved it. I had become a hustler. I would consider any job that allowed me time with my family.

I met Evelyn Lugo at a friend's party, and she told me she was a real estate agent. She also said she thought I would be good at it. I thought, "Why not?" I signed up for the courses, passed the exam, and got my license to become an agent. I learned so much in such a short time. For me, it was the perfect job. Peyton was now in preschool and thriving.

I would head to work after dropping the kids off at school and scoop them up at the end of the day. I could go on field trips, be the room parent, and volunteer at their school—all of the things I could never do working in a newsroom. It wasn't until my son was about to graduate from high school and my daughter was in middle school that I decided I really didn't love real estate. I enjoyed helping people find their perfect home and I was making a lot of money but, overall, the job did not bring me joy. It felt like work. It was time for reinvention.

I decided I would no longer do things because I made a lot of money or because others thought it was the perfect job for me. I worked really hard to make sure every step I took was intentional on a path to fulfillment. But this time it wasn't so easy. As I got older and saddled with more responsibilities, I found I didn't have the luxury of making quick, impulsive decisions. I had to take time to think them through.

As I was thinking, I found a casting notice for a political TV drama. I remember the look on my husband's face when I told him I was going to audition for the part. I wasn't an actress, but I could be pretty dramatic.

The next morning I got dressed and headed over to the studio in Virginia. When I arrived, the woman sitting behind the desk asked which part I was there to read. I didn't really know which show I was auditioning for or which roles were available.

So, I told her that I didn't know.

She suggested that I look through the scripts and pick one.

I came across a role for a homeless woman. I passed on that one. Then I saw one for an anchorwoman. Jackpot! I was psyched! I knew how to play an anchorwoman. I sat with the other actors and waited to be called.

It happened. I was a little giddy because no one else knew I wasn't an actress and actually an anchorwoman. As I started to read the script in the teleprompter, the photographer tilted his head from behind the camera and said, "Wow, you're good."

When I finished, he asked if I could adlib a newscast about politics.

I said sure but, in my head, I thought, "Hell yes, that's what I've been doing for years."

For about a minute and a half I rattled off a newscast about the latest political drama and all of its players.

The photographer looked amazed and said, "Wow," again.

I walked out of that studio knowing I had the part.

It was months before the call came. When it came, I was asked if I would shave my head and was available for the entire month of October. I said no and yes. The call ended.

A few weeks later I got another call. This time the person congratulated me. I got an anchorwoman part on—get this—*House of Cards*.

I didn't confess this to them, but I will to you: I had never seen *House of Cards*. I had no clue what it was about. I spent the next few days binge-watching the show on Netflix. It's a dark and fascinating series, and I was super excited to play even a small role. I was even more excited when I received the scripts because that meant it was official.

I was called in a few days before the shoot to go through wardrobe. I rolled in with two suitcases of my own clothes. I tried on several outfits before they decided on my mustard-colored dress and a brown pinstriped blazer. I packed up everything else and rolled out to my car.

On the day of the shoot, I was up and out early. I didn't want to be late. I knew where to go because it wasn't far from wardrobe. I was told to park behind the building, but there was a space right in the front of the door. So, I parked there.

The building security guard had a list, and I wasn't on it. That couldn't be right. I explained that I was a principal actor, one with a speaking role. He asked me to take a seat in a room just off the lobby. As I was patiently waiting, showrunner Beau Willimon walked by, saw me, and asked why I was sitting there. He was incredibly kind and actually knew who I was. He walked me through the studio, along the way introducing me to Kevin Spacey, members of the crew, and anyone else we passed on the way. We walked by the barbecue joint, the airplane, and other sets I recognized from the show.

Then, we arrived at my trailer!

Yep! I had my own trailer with my name on it. It looked like someone wrote my name on a piece of tape and stuck it to the door. But it was still my name on the trailer! I could have gone home right then. I didn't need anything else. I was kicked back enjoying the moment when someone knocked on my trailer to walk me over to the hair and makeup trailer. It was a whirlwind of fun.

When I walked out hair and makeup, I had bulletproof hair and more makeup than I had ever worn. But I looked good. Back in my trailer, I sat and waited, and waited, and waited. Hours passed before I was called to the studio. I walked behind the anchor desk and took my seat. It was the perfect height. The lights were in the perfect position. The only minor issue was there was too much stuff on the anchor desk. I asked if I could give my input and suggested that we keep either the stack of papers or the iPad, the mug, and get rid of everything else.

After two reads I was done. I had spent the entire day there, and I was beat. I wasn't sure if I could make the hour plus ride home, but I did.

A few weeks later I was called back to do another episode. This time I knew where to park, and I headed straight to my upgraded trailer. It was bigger and more modern. My script was also much longer, and there were words I had never seen or heard before.

There was also another Black woman. She had on the same dress, color, and style. She was about my height and close to my complexion. When I walked, she walked. When I sat, she sat. Here I am trying to be the professional actor for another day, and she was unnerving me.

I finally asked her, "What character are you playing?"

She said, "I'm you."

That bothered me. I leaned over quietly, so as not to cause a scene on the set of *House of Cards*, and asked, "What do you mean?"

She said, "I play you. You're an actor, right?"

The nerve of her. Of course, I'm an actor. Why the hell was I there? Instead of saying that, I said, "I'm playing one today."

She went on to explain that all principals have a stand-in. Who knew? She was my stand-in. That's why the chair was in the perfect position, and the lights were in exactly the right position. She had been in the studio playing me since before the sun came up. My job, she explained, was to focus on my lines and become my character. Mind-frickin'-blown!

So, I focused on my script. I had been reading it for weeks and doing research on the words foreign to me. When I walked on set, actress and director Robin Wright was there. She was wonderful. We went over the script together and decided for continuity on pronunciation we would reach out to Beau. Beau put us in contact with the writer who went over the pronunciation of each difficult word.

Then, the moment came. My nerves were more than rattled. I had to read this long script with more than a dozen words I had just learned to pronounce moments ago. It was quiet on the set, then the countdown, then I was cued to talk. As I spoke, it felt like everyone was holding their breath. When I finished, there was a call to check the video, still holding our collective breath. I got a thumbs-up, then cheers and applause. The tension released. I left with one of those big, silly grins on my face. I had become an actor.

Leaving my job—or being forced to leave what I thought was my identity—opened my eyes to opportunities I never considered. I took risks that made my heart thump and my nerves rattle but left me with a feeling of joy. And I continued the path of being my authentic self—not being defined by a job or a title, touching others along the way, and changing and challenging the way that I and other women walk this earth. That moment that brings about change is different for everyone.

When you focus on your unique gifts and what you are passionate about, your impossible becomes possible. You'll love the life you live. So, get uncomfortable. Be open to new opportunities even if they don't fit with who you think you are. Do that thing you've been dying to do. Look for new ways to live your life with joy and meaning. The journey doesn't have to be difficult, but it must be started.

Don't diminish your dreams to meet your reality. Change what's wrong in your life to reach your dreams.

CHAPTER 8

SHOW UP—LIVE FEARLESSLY

I was built this way for a reason, so I'm going to use it.
—SIMONE BILES

Every day, when you wake up, you get to choose. You get to decide if today is the day you're going to show up. Showing up looks different for all of us. For some it may be putting one foot in front of the other, and that's all they can do to get unstuck. For others, it's disrupting the universe.

Rachel McKenzie is one of those people who wakes up ready to stir the pot. Rachel is the person you notice in a crowd. She's poised, confident, and not afraid to take a chance. She says it started with her mother who had a strong work ethic: "When it's instilled in you, you can't shy away from it. It also helps to shape and curve your life."

When Rachel was twelve years old, her cousins taught her to make hooch and wine. She mastered it in her bedroom at night. In the morning on her way to school, she sold it to the men on the street. Her entrepreneurial spirit was budding. After school, from sixth grade to high school, she worked in her single mother's beauty shop washing hair and sweeping floors. She would do anything and everything, and she knew education was the key.

Over time, she honed the skills and sharpened her focus from sweeping floors to Olympic dreams in college. She was an honor student on a full scholarship and a track star. Her focus was on being an Olympian until she was injured, but her injury didn't crush her spirit. It strengthened her drive.

From college to a corporate boardroom, she learned leadership and business skills. She moved to the next job, always successful and always the youngest at her level. Soon Rachel realized she didn't want to work for a boss. She was going to be her own boss. Rachel is an entrepreneur at heart and has her eyes on being a billionaire. There are not many Black billionaires and even fewer Black female billionaires. Rachel decided to be the one and let life play out from there.

Together, Rachel and her husband, her number one cheerleader, own more than three hundred acres of orange groves and sell their oranges to Tropicana. Their trucking company hauls for FedEx and the federal government. They also own a seasoning company and a winery.

"I think it's the rush and keeping up with the high energy," she says. "I actually thrive on that."

Her mantra is, "Today will be better than yesterday. Today has to be better than yesterday because tomorrow is yet to come. If I can wake up and live another day, I promise it will be better than today."

Rachel has an intense drive and clear focus. When I asked if she's living her purpose, she answered, "I strongly believe that I am, and that's because I know the many gifts I have. Those gifts are all centered and literally utilized for business building and building wealth. My husband and I are trying to do it also at its greatest level of getting it done."

She definitely gets it done with grace and gratitude. While she is a strong, successful Black women, she has had her share of struggles. Often, she has walked into her trucking company and the men wonder whose assistant she is, never thinking that she is the owner, their boss. "My tone is strong," she says. "My facial expressions are strong, and it comes across as though I'm angry or bitter. And that can cloud someone's judgment at the table sometimes. You can't see me while being too busy judging me."

Rachel believes it's important to be your own cheerleader and have a few more on your team. Your support group should include people who are already doing what you want to do. She says, "For the last six years, I've been centering myself around like-minded people, women and men who are on my level or above. Those are the people I want to spend the bulk of my time with when it comes to educating myself and staying ahead of the game. I don't want to just stay in the game, I want to stay ahead. You don't know what you don't know."

Rachel lives unselfishly, sharing what she knows to help others find their purpose.

"Just waking up, living in my passion, and unselfishly paying it forward to help others—to me that's how I see success," she says.

Rachel believes that to find meaning in life, change the way you think and be willing to take what she calls "necessary risks." She asks, "Is the end result to exceed your expectation of whatever your goal is, or is your end result to just meet your goal? If you start off thinking in that mindset, then you've already limited where you can go. So that's the first thing you have to do is change the way that you think, the way that you normally would do business, or the way that you normally would do anything in your life. Change that mindset."

Changing your mindset is an essential step, not just in work but in everything you do. Your mindset shapes how you see the world and, in some ways, how the world responds to you. Negative thoughts will bring negative actions. When you're thinking negative thoughts, figure out how to shift the focus to joy. Find the positive in all that you do. When you're stuck in traffic and running late, instead of getting anxious or upset, think of it as free time to clear your mind. Find your favorite radio station and rock out or tune into that audiobook you've been meaning to listen to. The next time you wake up frustrated that you must go to a job you hate, thank God that you woke up another day.

Life is short, so do all you can to stir the pot. My definition of stirring the pot: changing your beliefs, getting uncomfortable, and shaking things up to discover your authentic self.

Jalene Mack definitely does. With endless energy and a desire to do more, she wears multiple hats as an entertainment attorney, author, actor, playwright, and producer.

She says people often asks how she balances it all. "Learning what my gifts and talents are and understanding them, I realized they were all connected. That's why it's so easy to do. It sounds like a lot, but it comes as second nature to me. I still have a passion for it because it's all tied into storytelling."

Her work brings her joy; that's why it doesn't feel like work. But that was not always the case. Jalene knew she always wanted to be in entertainment. Her university didn't have a theater department, so she majored in political science. After she graduated, she says she hit a fork in the road: "I knew I wanted to pursue an entertainment career, but I also needed to pay the bills. So, my waitressing job was going to law school to be a lawyer. That's how I was going to sustain my career in arts and entertainment."

Jalene passed the bar, built a clientele, and continued to practice, but was always eyeing the entertainment industry. Her moment of clarity came one day while in court. She says, "I found myself sitting in court, loathing being there, looking at these lawyers saying, 'How do y'all do that?' As if I wasn't a part of them. To me, it felt like work. It felt like a job. It felt like all the stresses were associated with it, and it felt strange."

Jalene knew as early as grade school that entertainment was her passion. It just took her a while to make it happen.

She decided to marry her job with her passion. She goes on to say, "I had that clarity moment of what my purpose was career-wise, and I knew it was clearly focused on the arts and entertainment side because I would rather act for free then get paid five thousand dollars to do somebody's divorce."

Have you ever thought about merging your career with your side hustle? Or making your side hustle your career? Finding that good fit sometimes takes time. Be patient. Discovering your passion is worth the wait.

Jalene offers these life lessons. Surround yourself with people who have already achieved the success you're chasing.

Ignore the naysayers, the people who have failed to find their own passions. She says she never lets a person tell her who she needs to be or how she needs to act so they can feel comfortable. "When someone tries to discount your gift and tell you why you're wasting your time, your money, or whatever, then that's a problem with their comfort level, not yours."

Jalene adds taking care of your vessel is key: "Your body is what your gifts flow through. So, health and exercise are important. Have a connection to God, whether you're a religious fanatic or just a spiritual person. You must stay centered. That's what keeps us from making bad mistakes."

Take care of others and give freely. What goes out always comes back. When you unselfishly share your gifts with others, the rewards are endless.

Jalene really stepped into her gifts when she launched her nonprofit which provides free or low-cost workshops focused on the entertainment industry for children and young adults.

She says it's been one of her greatest joys. "As I started to do more to help others, I realized a lot more about the talents, the gifts, the power that I had in being me. I always felt like my superpower really was networking and connecting people and giving people access."

You are connecting with people every day. We're all a part of this great big world. Don't hold your talents and gifts too close to your chest. They're too precious to keep secret. Share them freely with an open heart and mind. I'm sure the rewards will flow in abundance.

CHAPTER 9

PHENOMENAL WOMAN: HEAR HER. SEE HER.

———

Become more of who you are.

—OPRAH WINFREY

On my journey through life, so many amazing women have crossed my path: sisters, daughters, mothers, millionaires, celebrities, and everyday people doing extraordinary things both big and small. As women, we may move a mountain then say, "Oh, that was nothing." A man may move pebbles and claim the mountain. Of course, I'm overgeneralizing and exaggerating just a bit, but I hope my point isn't lost. What if we moved that mountain then climbed to the top and danced? Then, climbed down and moved another mountain. What would that look like to our future selves? What would that feel like? Are you willing to give it a try?

We all meet phenomenal women throughout our lives who are moving mountains, whether personal or professional. Many are willing to share the lessons learned if asked. Some may even walk your journey with you. But you must hear them and see them.

How many times have you been introduced to someone, only to forget their name the second they say it? Well, you may have just let an opportunity slip by. People come and go in our lives for a reason. When you meet someone—anyone—be present. Hear them. See them.

In my twenty plus years as a journalist, I've knocked on more doors than I can count, not knowing who was on the other side. And more times than not, people opened their homes and their hearts, sharing their deepest, darkest secrets and their loftiest hopes and dreams. I recounted their stories and shared a few of my own. The journey wasn't always easy, but at each stop I did my best to make sure the person I was speaking with knew I heard them.

My journalism path would eventually collide with Oprah Winfrey's. Yes, I met Oprah, and not only did I meet her, I interviewed her. Our interaction was brief, but the lessons learned in a matter of minutes will last a lifetime.

Trust me, you can't cross paths with a living legend and be the same. Her words and wisdom changed me. What she said and how she said it left me hungry for more. My curiosity set me further down the path to find my purpose.

On that day, she said, "The intention to live your life on purpose—this is my biggest message. Have the intent to live your life purpose and not try to be like anyone else."

Oprah says if you are trying to be someone you're not, you will never become the person you are meant to be.

It was the spring of 2005; Oprah was hosting the *Live Your Best Life Tour* making a stop in Washington, DC. Five thousand tickets sold out within minutes for $185 a pop. Oprah touching down in DC was big news.

I didn't have a ticket and didn't have full access to the event, but I was dying to know how Oprah lived her best life. I decided I would do everything I could for a chance to ask Oprah. I reached out to everyone I knew who had some connection to Oprah. Again, not easy, but I was laser focused and eventually landed a spot in the press line.

There I stood across from thousands of mothers, daughters, sisters, and girlfriends of all ages and ethnicities who traveled near and far to line up at the crack of dawn for a moment with Oprah. When she finally stepped out of her SUV with her entourage, including her bestie Gayle King, the women jumped, shook, screamed, and some even cried.

She walked over to a few and gave each of the women she touched what they were waiting for. For some, it was tickets or an autograph. For others, it was hope or a handshake.

A Nigerian woman who was battling cancer and was supposed to be in the hospital said she was waiting to feel Oprah's spirit. She said Oprah is an inspiration to women all over the world.

I watched as she moved along the crowd and made her way over to the waiting cameras and microphones. I must admit I was a little nervous and was not quite ready for my moment. Ready or not, it came. I struggled to get my first question out, managing to ask, "What do you give to them?"

"I give myself. And the thing that everybody sees in me is a piece of themselves." She went on, "I mean, my God, if I ain't the living American Dream, who is?"

She *is* the living American Dream. As she talked, she reached way back to being raised and "colored" in Mississippi in the 1950s. Take a minute and think about what that means for a little Black girl.

Oprah's grandmother was a maid. Her grandmother told her to watch as she boiled laundry because one day it would be her work. The expectation was that Oprah would be a maid too. But she had another dream—a belief—and it was larger than the limits Mississippi placed on her.

"I think when I was ten years old," she said, "and saw Sydney Portier get out of a limousine and win the Academy Award in 1964, that said to me it is possible for a Black person to do that. So, I think what people see in me is the possibility of what can happen. I don't think I'm different or special. I think what I have been able to do very well is listen to my inner voice and be guided by a power other than myself."

I followed with, "A lot of people would disagree and say you are different and special."

She said, "Everybody's special."

I replied, "It's hard to find that. It's hard to tap into that."

She responded, "You know why it's hard? Because people are listening to their mommas, to their sisters, to their husbands, to their cousins, to their friends, to society, to the radio, to the MTV, to BET, to everything else, to the images. The way you become who you are meant to be is to listen to your inner voice that guides everybody. Everybody has it. That's why I say I'm not special. The difference between me and a lot of other people is that I'm obedient to my own calling. I'm obedient to my calling. That's the number one difference because everyone who obeys their own calling will get to the highest place they were meant to be in. You will fulfill your mission in life."

Oprah says as long as you are pretending to be something you are not or you accept other's opinion of you, you will never become who you are meant to be.

You'll know when you're living your authentic self. You'll discover your personal flow—that ultimate state of happiness and fulfillment, life's balance. Your new magnetic presence will draw people to you.

Oprah has touched millions, and she has proven time and again wherever she goes, they will follow. She has engendered trust among women of the world, talking to them as if they're chatting one woman to another. She publicly celebrates her victory and exposes her mistakes. She says, "I don't feel pressure. I feel like life is one big, wonderful, adventurous experience and there is no such thing as failure. You learn from your mistakes, and you pick yourself up, and you say don't do that again."

Talking to Oprah, I felt like she saw me and she heard me. It didn't matter thousands were waiting for her both outside and inside the Washington Convention Center that day. She gave me her time, her attention, and as much wisdom as she could squeeze into our minutes together.

After our interview ended, I had just a moment to talk to her best friend Gayle King, a phenomenal woman in her own right. The author and broadcast journalist was there to talk about her friend, saying, "What's phenomenal to me is to see how Oprah touches people just by being herself. It's not like she gets up and tries to have a good plan or what can I say today to try to inspire or teach people. She inspires, leads, and teaches people just by living her life and being herself."

Oprah may disagree, but I think that's pretty special. And like Oprah, I believe our real job on this earth is to find our calling and figure out a way to live it. We all have it in us. We all have the power to fulfill our life's mission.

Oprah's words and wisdom seeped into my soul and empowered me to continue my journey of being the best me I am meant to be.

Over the years, my life has changed because of that quick chat with Oprah. I've learned to give without expecting anything in return. It's important to own who you are. I've mastered the art of saying no, and, in fact, it's empowering. I don't let people tell me who I am. I recover quickly from mistakes and appreciate the lessons learned. And I understand that I am still a work in progress.

What about you? Are you ready to share your lessons learned? Do you even know what they are? What can you do today, this week, to begin your journey of finding your gifts, sharing them with the world, and living your purpose?

Don't wait for the perfect time to make a change. There is no perfect time. Get comfortable with the fact that you are a phenomenal woman. Start living in your power.

I hear you. I see you.

CHAPTER 10

SET IT ON FIRE!

You wanna know what scares people? Success.
When you don't make moves and when you
don't climb up the ladder, everybody loves
you because you're not competition.

—NICKI MINAJ

About halfway through writing this book, I had an emotional breakdown. It only lasted a couple of hours, but that was more than enough. It was the morning I woke up knowing that something was off. I couldn't put my hands on it, but I knew. I was a little weepy and exhausted, not ready to face the day. I leaned on everyone I knew, all my close friends, the people who knew me well, and those who knew I was writing a book. I wanted just one of them to tell me it was too much and that I should stop writing. I wanted them to say that this book was just too big of a task.

I don't know if you've ever written a book, but the task is monumental. It is not always a fun process. And I know some would say it's a horrible process. Self-doubt follows you throughout the journey. If you just crack open that door of doubt, all of the questions start flooding in. Am I good enough? Will anyone read this book? Will they like it? Will the book be good enough? Who am I to tell this story? Imposter syndrome is a real thing.

"I can't do it. I'm overwhelmed. It's just too much," I said as I stood in the loving embrace of my husband.

He silently held me because he knew no matter what he said, they would be the wrong words. When he did speak, he calmly suggested I take a nap, and then we could talk afterward.

Well, hell, I didn't want to take a damn nap. It wasn't time to take a nap. I wanted him to agree with me—that I should stop writing this book and that it was the right thing to do.

But instead, he said, "You can meet your deadline. You can get this done."

That was the spark I needed to return to the keyboard. I realized I had been so focused on sparking a flame for everyone else, I forgot I needed to keep my own fire going. Sometimes we really are our worst enemy.

This experience reminded me of a conversation I had with actor and entrepreneur Kiana Dancie. She's a self-professed fussing, cussing comedienne who knows the Lord. Her faith keeps her grounded. Her sense of humor keeps her moving. Kiana delivers part sermon, part comedy, and a whole lot of inspiration. She proclaims the power of a woman, "Nine times out of ten, the woman is the glue. She's the gas. She's the fuel. If she stops, everything else stops. You can't stop. When you need a day, take your day. But in that day, you need to take time and look yourself in the mirror and remind yourself who you are. Look at you. You are amazing. You're fantastic. You affirm you."

Unabashed and unapologetic, quitting is not an option for Kiana. She replaced the words *try*, *can't*, and *maybe* with *can*, *will*, and *did*. I can. I will. I did.

"Over and over again, I fight for the right to be in the room," she says. "Even when there's not a chair for me at the table, that's alright. I'll be back. I'll go grab my own chair."

The strongest struggles birth the greatest rewards. They define who we are and who we will be.

Kiana says, "I am who I am because of what I've been through."

She has been through both joy and pain. Kiana survived child molestation and trauma as a teenager. An unimaginable moment long ago when she was seventeen years old left its mark on Kiana. Her boyfriend was shot in front of her in her mother's house.

"If your life is anything like mine, there are so many reasons to give up." Kiana continues, "But, when you think about all of the things God has done for you, for me and the people around us, there are so many reasons to keep going. I just don't give up. I keep pushing."

No matter how bad you think your past is or how awful the memories may be, you can get through it. Kiana offers the words she lives by: "Set fire to the thing that's holding you hostage. Set fire to everything that's held you back. Set fire to everything that tells you no. But, set ablaze your future. Set ablaze your possibilities."

Kiana set her past on fire and is looking toward a bright future. She knows her purpose and believes it is forever changing. Kiana has her own business, has hosted a television show, and is writing a book. She's still headlining shows and making audiences laugh.

The energy her advice emits is priceless. Setting your past on fire can ease the guilt, the shame, and even the grief. It can also banish imposter syndrome. It frees you to walk in your own light.

If you could set your past on fire, what would you burn? Who would you forget? Why not do it now? Give yourself permission to forget past woes—all the things and the people who are holding you back. Set your past on fire and free your mind to think beyond.

Get out of your own head and take the first step in believing that anything really is possible. That dream you've been having—make it real. The idea you've been thinking about forever—make it happen.

According to Jim Kwik, the world-famous brain coach, the biggest mistake he sees people making is downgrading their dreams. His advice: "Do not shrink what's possible to fit your mind. Expand your mind to fit what's possible." His prescription for getting those juices flowing is to do something mental and physical every day. Read a book or write in a journal. Take a walk or work out. Create habits, starting with a morning routine that consists of things you're not accustomed to doing like taking a cold shower or brushing your teeth with your left hand.

You are the greatest gift you get to work on. So today, get to work creating your own magic. That first step may appear difficult, but that step opens the opportunity of wonders.

It's what entrepreneur Tomasina (Tommy) Boone has been doing her whole life. Tommy gives credit to her mom who gave her "the freedom to live, to dream, and to move forward," she says.

And move she did, but not down the block or to another state. Tommy and her family packed up, left New York, and moved more than ten thousand miles away to Australia. She left home and everything she knows. That big adventure changed her life.

"What changed me here is that I had a moment to quiet the noise. And, as women, if we can take the time to quiet the noise around us, I believe we will hear our true voices. Listening [to your true voice] will lead you to the path you're supposed to be on, but you need a little silence to hear it."

Silence gave her clarity and set her mission in motion.

So many of us are stuck, confined by our current circumstances. For Tommy, leaving America and changing her environment relieved her mental obligations and gave her the freedom to explore life and take chances. Today, Tommy is driving the curly hair movement in Australia as one of the biggest importers of hair products for women with curls.

At the time of writing this book, Tommy is running other businesses, working on a beauty app, and helping start a foundation. She's brought together women of all ethnic and cultural backgrounds, and she's not done. Tommy says she's doing what was done for her. She's standing on the shoulders of those who gave her guidance.

She's giving the same guidance to her daughters. Since they were born, she's been helping them explore what excites them. She formed a group with her girls and a few other eleven-to-fourteen-year-old girls to help them discover the person they want to become. She says it's about girls living their life on purpose. "We stopped encouraging young girls to live the recipe but to live their purpose. What they want to do. What makes them happy. What makes them get out of bed. Starting the conversation now instead of when they're twenty-five."

She's exposing the girls to stock portfolios, art, cooking, business building, and more. They create vision boards and hear from professionals. They discuss haircare, skincare, and the importance of friendship.

"Just trying to give them the tools that we all need to help us live freely," Tommy says.

She often tells her girls, "I'm going to tell you now; you'll hear me later." Tommy shares the lessons now in hopes that they will put them to use later. She hopes her guidance and the lessons they learn today will help them live lives full of meaning.

Imagine if you were exposed to all the possibilities of living freely at such a young age. Would your life be different? Well, it's never too early to start and, definitely, never too late. Your reality is steeped in your beliefs. Change what you believe, and you'll change how you live.

Give yourself permission to listen to your internal calling. And, when you're done, all those things people told you are impossible—make them possible. Why? Because you can.

CHAPTER 11

TRUST YOUR INNER VOICE

——

I'm no longer accepting the things I cannot change.
I'm changing the things I cannot accept.

—ANGELA DAVIS

There were days when it was nearly impossible to get out of bed, to put one foot in front of the other. I would wake up in a fog, barely able to focus. I felt a heavy weight on my shoulders, and my head was cloudy. I would push through day after day not because I could but because I had to. My family needed me. My clients needed me. It didn't matter that my body seemed to be giving out.

I went through almost a year of medical discovery. I had an MRI of my head, hoping the scans didn't discover a brain tumor. I did an ultrasound of my liver, my stomach, and my adrenal glands. I wanted the test results to reveal the reason I had no energy and couldn't think clearly.

I had visited my internist first then headed over to my gastroenterologist. When that was not enough, I went to my cardiologist. I kept going, trying to figure out what was wrong. I went to doctor after doctor searching for answers. I should have been ecstatic when they told me everything looked normal. Instead, I was frustrated, even angry. I knew something was off. I know my body better than anyone, even my doctors. I just couldn't figure it out. Even though I started to feel better, I was still bothered because I can usually diagnose my problems or, at least, pinpoint the illness.

Many years ago when I was breastfeeding my son, I found a tiny pea-sized lump in my breast. It wasn't deep down inside.

It laid right at the surface. I went to an oncologist to have it checked out. She told me that it was just a cyst, and I shouldn't worry about it.

It was still there a year later, so I requested a mammogram and an ultrasound to see if there was anything usual. The male radiologist told me it was just a cyst. I asked if I should get a biopsy to make sure. He looked at me incredulously and asked, "Why would you cut into healthy tissue?" For years, I vacillated between what I knew in my gut was a problem and the possibly of cutting into healthy flesh. It was not until my son was about ten years old and my mother had died from complications of breast cancer that I decided the small bump had to go. The skin around it had turned purple and was sunken like a dimple on the surface of my right breast. There was no pain. Just anxiety.

I became even more vigilant. I kept going to doctor after doctor finally visiting my dermatologist, Dr. Emily Gerson. She told me that it could be one of two things: a protuberance or a bug that had burrowed into my skin and died. Regardless, she said it should be removed. Hearing those words erupted an emotional volcano somewhere inside me. Tears that pooled slowly streamed my face. Then, the sobbing started. I was so relieved that someone could finally hear me and see me. I was relieved that the tiny bump was going to be removed.

I made an appointment with an oncologist and anxiously waited for the day to arrive. When I walked into the office, I looked around a waiting room I had never seen before and took my seat waiting to see a doctor I didn't know. The nurse called my name. I don't remember the walk back to the examination room. I do remember telling the doctor I wanted him to cut out the bump. The doctor took one look at the sunken, purple area on my breast and told me that it should be removed and that he could do it now. I must confess I wasn't expecting him to say he could do it now. For so many years doctors told me it was normal skin, it was just a cyst, or something along those lines. Believe me, I definitely wanted it out. I just wasn't prepared for someone to cut me at that moment. Still, I knew deep down that it was the right decision, so I decided to do it.

I'm no fool. Someone needed to know I was getting cut. I called Roy, my husband. I gave him the quick and dirty rundown of the conversation with the doctor and the doctor's name, address, and phone number. I told him if I didn't call him within the hour to come get me.

It was time. As I laid on the table, the doctor numbed the area then carefully sliced into my breast. He cut around and under the small bump. As he looked closer, he uttered, "Ew." You never want anyone to pull anything out of your body and say "Ew." After that, I had to see it.

The doctor had already put it in a bottle with liquid in it. He handed it to me. I looked at it as closely as I could. It was an oddly shaped, brown ball of flesh, flat on the top with a small ball of fat on the bottom. Extending from the bottom fatty part was what I could only describe as little legs. There were dozens of tiny legs. It was gross and fascinating at the same time. Worst of all, it came out of me.

I asked the oncologist what it was. He said he didn't know. I asked why part of it was brown. He said whatever it was it wouldn't let go of my skin, so he had to cut a part of my brown skin to remove the bump. He sent it to a lab that specialized in skin disorders. The results would be back in about a week. The wait was agonizing. I'm normally a pretty positive, glass-half-full person. But, deep down, I knew the news wouldn't be good.

When the results finally arrived, it was like a punch in the face. I had cancer. Not just cancer, a very rare cancer that not many people know about. It's called dermatofibrosarcoma protuberans, DFSP for short. I didn't know much about it. My internist didn't either. None of my doctors did. I spent days researching and, again, going from doctor to doctor, to discuss my best course of action.

I even reached out to a good friend who is a dermatologist in Cleveland. The cancer is so rare, with only about one thousand cases in the United States each year, that he was convinced that the lab made a mistake. He asked me to send him the lab results, and he would forward them to the person who specializes in rare skin cancers. He called me as soon as he received the reports. Apparently, that specialist did do my labs. I definitely had DFSP.

DFSP is a rare skin cancer. It has tentacles that can grow around fat, tissue, and even bone. Doctors say it can disfigure you. In my case, the tentacles were growing towards my rib cage. Thankfully, it was slow growing and had not reached that point. It had to be removed and every doctor offered different ways to get it done. A top doctor who specializes in breast cancer said I should remove the entire breast and have reconstructive surgery. Another doctor told me to remove part of the breast and have reconstructive surgery. A third doctor, a dermatologic surgeon, offered Mohs surgery. It's also what my friend in Cleveland recommended.

I went with Mohs surgery. The Skin Cancer Foundation describes Mohs surgery: "The procedure is done in stages, all in one visit, while the patient waits between each stage. After removing a layer of tissue, the surgeon examines it under a microscope in an on-site lab. If any cancer cells remain, the surgeon knows the exact area where they are and removes another layer of tissue from that precise location, while sparing as much healthy tissue as possible. The doctor repeats this process until no cancer cells remain."
(Skin Cancer Foundation)

My surgery was done in the doctor's office. It lasted about four hours, and I was awake with Roy in the room the entire time. Nurses prepped the area and put up a tissue-thin sheet so I couldn't see the procedure. After a few hours of cutting and waiting, I was starving. I asked the surgeon if I could go out for lunch. Do you know? He said yes! He actually packed the hole in my chest, bandaged me up, and sent me out. I had to promise to return when he called. We had a lovely lunch and were just finishing when I got the call to return.

He completed the surgery and told me the margins were clear, the tentacles were gone. For the rest of my life, I would have to return to my doctor every six months to a year to be examined because the cancer has a high recurrence rate.

To this day, that experience still makes me tear up. I think we all have those moments when we know deep in our gut that something is off. Call it intuition or trusting your inner voice. I've experienced it more times than I can recall. I have even witnessed others doing it as well.

I remember a time when my then eighty-one-year-old dad trusted his inner voice and possibly saved his own life. That day started out as any other day. The alarm went off at 6:30 a.m., which is always way too early. I hit snooze to catch another five minutes. I promise those five minutes make a difference—at least, that's what I like to believe. I made sure my daughter Peyton was up and getting dressed for school. She's incredibly independent but sometimes needs that extra push in the morning. She packed her lunch the night before. We grabbed breakfast and were out the door at 7:15 a.m.

Peyton threw her backpack on the backseat just as she was getting into the car. There it sat perched on the edge of the seat. I saw it rocking just as I was getting in, thinking I should probably straighten it out, but I didn't. We pulled out of the driveway and were on our way to school. Because of the pandemic, my daughter's school was on a hybrid schedule. The school split each grade into two groups: cohort A and cohort B. Cohort A went to school when cohort B stayed home studying virtually. The next week they would switch. Cohort A claimed Peyton, and this was their week to have in-person classes.

Just as we were getting on the highway, her backpack tumbled off the seat. At that moment, my phone rang. I hate getting those early-morning calls because they are rarely good. This one was bad. It was my dad calling.

There was a time when he would call me early in the morning just to say good morning and I love you. Now, early-morning calls announce an emergency. And this was an emergency. I answered the phone, "Hello." My dad said, "I'm having a stroke."

He had already called my sister, Tanya, who is in New Orleans with him. It didn't take long for Tanya to call 911 and a friend who lived nearby. On that day, New Orleans was facing a fierce ice storm, the worst it had seen in years. The roads were iced over, and driving was a nightmare but somehow, someway, someone had to help my father.

The whole time I was on the phone with my father. He kept asking who is coming? Is Tanya coming? She wasn't, but I told him she was. I didn't want him to worry about anything. He was already worried that no one would be there to open the door. He was right. The roads were too icy for anyone to drive to his house. He would have to open the door when the paramedics arrived.

It took the paramedics eighteen minutes to get there. They were trying to ring the doorbell that had been broken for years. My dad didn't know they were outside. They called my sister, who then called me.

I said to my dad, "The paramedics are outside, and, dad, minutes matter. We have a friend coming; she's three minutes away. Dad, minutes do matter. You can wait for her, or we can try to get you to the door."

He said, "I will try."

I said, "Stay on the phone with me, and stand up."

He stood up saying, "I'm standing."

I asked him if he could walk. He said, "I don't know."

I told him, "Take one step and fall back into the chair if you have to."

He took a step.

He said, "I think I can make it."

It was a slow walk to the door. As I sat on the phone listening to his shuffled steps, my heart was pounding. I hoped with every ounce of my being that he would make it. I would not be able to bear the sound of him hitting the floor knowing that help was on the other side of the door. Time seemed to crawl. When he finally made it to the door, he slurred his words saying, "I'm at the door, but I can't open it."

In a matter of minutes, the stroke had affected his speech and paralyzed his left arm. He is a leftie. I told him to put the phone down and try with his other hand. That hand was weaker than usual, but he was able to open the door. He never picked up the phone, but I stayed on listening to the paramedics work with him. I heard him answering questions and knew that he was headed to the hospital and would get the care he needed.

What struck me that day was how well he knew his body. Long after he left the hospital and was going through physical therapy to regain movement on his left side, I asked him, "Dad, how did you know you were having a stroke?" His thought process was a little slower. He eventually said, "I got up to fix my breakfast"—you don't make breakfast in New Orleans, you fix it—"and the pot slid out of my hand. I knew at that moment that I was having a stroke."

He didn't feel any pain. He just went with his gut and called me and my sister moments after the pan hit the kitchen floor. It may have saved his life. It definitely slowed the effects of the stroke. After just a few weeks of physical therapy, he was able to lift his left arm and grasp things with his left hand.

It's amazing that my eighty-one-year-old father listened to his inner voice and knew exactly what his body was telling him.

It's something we can all do. We've been living and growing in our own bodies since the moment of our being. No one knows you better than you. So, when is the last time you listened to your inner voice? When did you last follow your gut? Don't doubt your instincts. Trust your inner voice.

Here's an exercise. The next time you go to the store, and you pull out the list of things you know you need, every time you eye something that's not on the list, but your gut tells you to get it, do it. Buy the item and see what happens. I bet when you get home, you'll realize that you need it. It may be the ingredient missing from a dish you are planning to whip up for dinner or something your child needs for school. I have been going with my gut for years, and it's never steered me wrong. Try it and let me know how it works out.

It gets even better if you pay attention to your inner voice in the shower. It may sound crazy, but I birth many of my most creative ideas in the shower. As the hot water pelts my body, these big, magnificent shower thoughts tumble forth. I'm sure these stories I cook up have always been there, but they seem so much more vivid in the rainfall of the shower. I probably dream about them at night, but when I wake up in the morning—nothing new. However, when I'm enclosed in that glass box, not only are my creative juices overflowing, but they're also bubbling up to the surface and forcing me in action. Epiphanies hatch so quickly that when my husband asked what I wanted for Christmas, I said a shower recorder because as I'm toweling off some of those big ideas start to dry up too.

I wondered if I'm crazy or if other people's creativity flows in the shower. Turns out, it's actually a thing. Many people have some of their biggest and best ideas in the shower. It's even backed up by science. It seems that our brains will come up with great thoughts when we relax, which makes sense since taking a shower is relaxing. Some blame it on dopamine, a neurotransmitter. Your body makes it. It's sometimes called a chemical messenger because your nervous system uses it to send messages between cells. It's directly related to motivation, focus, and enjoyment. Apparently, when we take showers our bodies relax and produce more dopamine. There are skeptics who say it's the lack of distraction that allows our creative juices to flow.

Regardless, cognitive psychologist Scott Barry Kaufman, PhD, proved that shower thoughts are a real thing. He conducted a study that shows that 72 percent of the people surveyed experienced more new ideas in the shower than they do at work. In fact, 14 percent of them take showers just to get those creative thoughts and big ideas. (Kaufman, 2014)

So, the next time you have a difficult problem or you have writer's block, jump in the shower and relax. Escape from the noise and let your inner voice flow. It may be the only moment in a hectic day where you can let your mind wander and daydream. Just make sure you have something nearby to capture those thoughts when they happen.

As I dug a little deeper, I found that shower thoughts are talked about all over the internet. They're a thing. Reddit even has an entire subreddit on them. Here are a few of the more popular ones:

"When you're a kid, you don't realize you're also watching your mom and dad grow up." (Reddit, 2019)

"Night before a day off is more satisfying than the actual day off." (Reddit, 2019)

"Biting your tongue while eating is a perfect example of how you can still screw up, even with decades of experience." (Reddit, 2020)

"Growing up is realizing you get more joy out of seeing others open presents than you do from opening your own." (Reddit, 2020)

Showers are not your thing? No worries. Turns out, you can find creative inspiration by doing anything that frees your mind—think sleeping, exercising, walking, even driving. It's amazing what can happen when you relax and clear the mental noise. Just be sure to trust your inner voice. It will likely lead you on an incredible journey.

CHAPTER 12

STANDING STRONG

———

You may not control all the events that happen to you, but you can decide not to be reduced by them.

—MAYA ANGELOU

According to the American Psychological Association, "The process of adapting well in the face of adversity, trauma, tragedy, threats, or significant sources of stress" is resilience. Those difficult experiences don't have to break us down. We can bounce back, recover, and even learn from them. Resilience gives you the courage to keep moving forward. (Palmiter, Alvord, Dorlen, Comas-Diaz, Luthar, Maddi, O'Neill, Saakvitne, Tedeschi, 2012)

We're not born with resilience. It's learned. It's like working out and building muscle. It takes time to build up your resilience. So, when are you going to start? How are you going to respond to adversity? Will you be a victim or a survivor? You can't always control what happens to you, but you can decide how you will respond.

I was about five years old living in New Orleans with my family when I had my first lesson in resilience. My sister Tanya and I road with my parents as we searched for a new house. We looked at several houses—ones with an indoor swimming pool, big yards, fancy kitchens, you name it. I wanted the house with the pool, but my mother quickly pointed out that I couldn't swim. A minor detail.

We ended up buying the most beautiful house I had ever seen. I had my own room, and it was right next to my sister's. My parents had their own bathroom. We all had to share a bathroom at our last house. The kitchen floors were terrazzo. The screened-in patio showed off a huge backyard blanketed in lush green grass. A grill built out of bricks the same color of the house was perfect for those parties my parents threw every Friday night. The neighborhood was really quiet. What I didn't realize then was that we were the first Black family in an all-white neighborhood. However, I quickly became woke.

It was the holiday season and the first Christmas in our new home. On that day, the Christmas cheer was running high. My mom was drinking her eggnog. She was the only one in the house who liked eggnog. My sister and I were decorating the tree. Dad hung the lights outside. We went to sleep with smiles on our faces, counting down the days to Christmas.

The next morning, as we walked out the front door on our way to school, we first noticed our Christmas lights on the ground. My dad thought it was odd because it hadn't been a particularly windy night. When we looked closer, we saw the lights had been slashed. But who would do that? And why was there so much red paint on the ground? It was everywhere but most noticeably on our sidewalk and driveway where someone had spray painted the word "Niggers." I stood there wondering if it was spray paint or blood. I didn't understand what was happening or why my parents were pushing us back into the house. My dad went back outside to see if there was any more destruction. There was. Our white German shepherd dog, Snow, was dead. Someone had killed him and left his body on the side of the house. We never even heard him whimper.

Everything changed that day. Our affluent neighborhood was no longer safe. We had moved up right into the hands of hatred. Our home became our fortress, and I really couldn't go outside, not even to the patio by myself. That was the ultimate punishment for a young child who could see the huge yard but couldn't roll around in the green grass that was as thick as a shag rug, whip up mud pies after a classic New Orleans torrential storm, or build a fort with downed branches in the yard. Our reality changed.

We never found out who did it. I don't remember the police being called. I remember facing a newfound fear while my mother found the strength to stand a little straighter, hold her head a little higher. She may have been scared, but she never showed it. Grace under pressure. Resilient. She didn't focus on being a victim. Her focus was on protecting her family and surviving. She pulled from an inner strength and sought support from family.

From then on, every day after school, the bus would drop us off at our grandparents' house in uptown New Orleans. We'd head inside, do our homework, have our snack, and play for hours until my mom arrived from work to pick us up. The majority of the families in their neighborhood were Black, so it was considered safe for my sister and I to play outside. It was a retreat from racism. I was even allowed to cross Louisiana Avenue Parkway to play with my friends: Michelle, Patrice, and Nicole.

My grandmother mastered afterschool snacks. Lima beans were my sister's favorite, as were beets with onions and vinegar, and my favorite was homemade biscuits. My grandmother made everything delicious. I still have memories of my grandmother's flour-caked hands putting the worn cookie sheet in the oven. I would sit impatiently watching the biscuits rise. When they were ready, she'd take them out, smother them with butter and molasses, and warn us to "be careful, they're hot." Those biscuits would melt in your mouth. She never had a written recipe to pass down. I've been trying to recreate those little bites of heaven for years. They, along with my grandmother's tender hugs, provided comfort on those difficult days.

Her recipes came straight from her own mother's kitchen in Stampley, Mississippi, where she was born and raised. Word had it she and my grandfather had to flee Stampley in the dark of night. The neighbor's dog had been hunting and killing my grandfather's chickens. He asked the neighbor time and time again to control his dog. Finally, he told the neighbor if it happened again, he would save his chickens. Well, it happened again, and, as the story goes, my grandfather shot the dog and saved the chickens. A Black man shooting a white man's dog in the 1930s was a death sentence. My grandparents fled, heading to New Orleans where they raised their three girls and doted on their grandchildren after school.

The days spent with our grandparents were worry free and comforting. I didn't have to worry that hate was lurking on my doorstep. If my grandparents were not watching over me, I knew someone was, either the neighbors or my Cousin Bit. Her real name was Mary Swanson, but everyone called her Cousin Bit because she was petite. She moved in with my grandparents after Aunt Bernice, my grandfather's aunt, died. Cousin Bit was blind. She lost sight when she was in the second grade but, somehow, she always knew what was going on. She knew the neighbors and their kids. She walked around the house with dark glasses on, and, as kids, we wondered if she could see because she never bumped into walls or slowed down as she rounded the corner.

She was older than my grandfather, but in my young eyes she was the perfect playmate. I would sit and ask Cousin Bit countless questions. If you're blind, how do you know colors? When did you become blind? Why are your eyes that color? Do you walk into walls? How do you know someone is in the room? She patiently answered question after question, even the silly ones. And, when she got tired of my questions, she tried to teach me how to read braille or would ask me to read my book to her.

Cousin Bit was my second lesson in resilience. Here was a woman, in her sixties at the time, who managed to outlive her brothers, aunts, and cousins. She lost her sight but never stopped learning. She never stopped believing that every day was an opportunity to do more.

One day, when everyone was out, Cousin Bit heard someone trying to break into the house. She may have been blind, but that woman could hear a dust bunny roll across the floor. She heard the old window in the guest bedroom whining as it was slowly pushed up the frame. Cousin Bit felt the warm, humid air rush in and the paralyzing fear knowing the intruder was entering the house. She couldn't run. She didn't know how to use the phone. So, she just screamed. She screamed so loud, the neighbor in the yard next door knew something was wrong. Apparently, the intruder knew too. Cousin Bit could hear him quickly backing out of the window. We never found out who it was, but Cousin Bit was sure it was our neighbor's son.

My third lesson in resilience came when I was in high school. Most of the time, I rode the public bus to my grandparents' house. Occasionally, I rode the bus to my own house. It didn't happen often, but when I did, I was usually with two or three friends until I transferred to the next bus. I was on that bus with one other friend. She got off a few stops before me.

One day, as I got off the bus and headed home, I noticed a car easing up behind me. I quickened my steps, but the car moved faster. Then, it was right at my side. That was when I heard them, the words. "UGLY. BLACK BITCH. NIGGER."

We all know the saying, "Sticks and stones may break my bones, but words will never hurt me." So not true. Each word dealt its own blow. They cut through my heart like a knife. Those words spewed from their lips like vomit. I picked up my steps, afraid that if I ran they would give chase. I didn't know who it was. I was too scared to look.

The awful names kept coming. My heart raced, and my head spun. Three blocks down, one block to go. My house was so close. I knew I could make it, even if I had to run. That gave me the courage to beat down my fears and look my attackers in the eyes. They were boys, teenagers just like me but older, white, and filled with hate. That carload of young, white boys followed me to my doorstep, yelling the worst words I had ever heard in my entire life.

My hands shook as I reached up to insert the key in the door. It wasn't until I was safely locked behind my iron door, the one installed to keep us safe in our own home, that I collapsed and cried. Sitting on the ground between that iron door and the wooden door, I sobbed. I made it safely inside.

As I tried to calm my shaking, I remembered our first Christmas when our home was vandalized, and our dog was killed. Years later, the attacks were still coming. We didn't have cell phones. I couldn't call for help.

Once inside, I called my mother from the phone attached to the wall in our kitchen. I leaned on that wall and told her the details of that difficult walk home. As always, she was my comfort and my strength. On that horrible day, I feared for my life. I still haven't forgotten it or the way I felt. But it didn't define me or determine my future. I pulled from my inner strength and found the courage and resilience to be like my mom, to stand up a little straighter and hold my head up a little higher.

I'm not sure where that strength comes from. Maybe it comes from all the wounds healed from horrible experiences that are now memories and scars. But in the face of fear, I am able to find clarity and focus. I can see beyond the situation to find the solution. No matter how big or how bad it is, I'm ready for the fight. I have always believed I will come out okay on the other side. Like NASA administrator Charles Bolden says, "It's not the size of the dog in the fight. It's the size of the fight in the dog."

So, how do you build your resilience? Find purpose. Studies have shown that people who have a sense of purpose are better able to bounce back and recover after being knocked down. Some people will argue that finding their purpose is actually harder than building resilience. But, finding your purpose doesn't have to be a daunting task, and it doesn't have to be focused on just one thing. Your purpose is always changing, always evolving.

Ask yourself these questions:

What makes you giddy, totally full of joy—that thing you would do for free? When you're doing it, you totally lose track of time. You could do it all day and never get tired of it.

What are your natural skills—those things you do easily? Where do you feel you can make a difference?

CHAPTER 13

A MOTHER'S COURAGE

I knocked on her door ever so slightly, hoping she didn't hear me and hoping with all my heart that she didn't answer the door. But she heard me, and she answered. A grieving mother, with tear-stained cheeks on that grieving day welcomed me inside her home. It was so peaceful, an eerie calm. She invited me to sit next to her on the sofa. I wasn't a mother yet, but I could feel her grief seep into my soul.

It was the late 1990s, and I was a reporter on assignment for WGHP TV in High Point, North Carolina. My photographer and I were sent to talk to the family of a little girl who had died earlier that day. When the mother answered the door, I asked my photographer to stay back and to not record the moment. I even told the mother that she didn't have to talk to us and probably shouldn't.

She invited me in anyway and talked about her daughter. She had left for school that day, riding the school bus with the other neighborhood children. Sometime during that day, she got into an argument with her longtime friend, another little neighbor girl who also rode the school bus home. When they were getting off the bus, the girl's friend pushed her. That little girl, a mother's child, fell under the bus just as it was pulling away. The little girl couldn't get up to make it home. The bus crushed her. Some of the kids saw. Some of the kids heard. The neighbors were there.

I don't know who told the mother. I don't know when they told her. By the time I got there, as I was sitting next to her, it was clear that she knew. Her daughter wasn't coming home.

I had gotten used to covering stories about grieving mothers and stories about people who have died and talking to the family, friends, and neighbors they left behind. I had done it countless times as a local news reporter. But this was horrible, unbearable. It has stayed with me for years, as have the mother's words.

Her eyes filled with tears as she looked at me. She said, "Every day I give my daughter to God, and today He decided to keep her." That mother, who was living a nightmare, somehow showed a level of strength, courage, wisdom, or whatever you want to call it that was unfathomable. Her raw emotions, her strength, and her sadness have stayed with me all these years.

Life isn't easy, and I'm not sure that it's supposed to be. It is precious and, unfortunately, too short. We will all struggle. But through struggle, hopefully we find the strength and spark to climb out of our own sadness or our own challenges. I have come to rely on that mother's courage when I am faced with my own trauma.

One of the toughest times of my life is when I realized my own mother was dying, when I knew deep down in my soul that she would leave me soon.

It's been more than a decade, and I still can't talk about my mother's battle with breast cancer without my chest tightening and my eyes watering. My mother was my everything. My base. My support. My comfort. My love. My world. She was an amazing woman with a sharp tongue and a hearty laugh. She was a loyal friend, a protective mother, and a kind soul.

The day she called to tell me about her diagnosis, I was in Washington, DC, covering the disappearance of Washington intern Chandra Levy. I walked away from the story and dropped everything. Friends packed my bags and bought me a plane ticket. I was at the airport boarding a plane to New Orleans within two hours of her call.

When I arrived at her house, my house, she opened the door and said, "I knew you were coming." We were somehow always connected. She knew what I was feeling before I told her. We talked every day, sometimes several times a day. If I had good news, I called her. If I had bad news, I called her. Even when I had no news, I called my mother, my best friend.

My mother was smart and independent and, at the same time, funny and kind. She took in children whose mothers were not able to raise them. She picked up elderly women who didn't have a ride to church. When my parents divorced, she took on a part-time job so my sister and I could stay at our private school. She was the strongest woman I have known. She was my superwoman, and I was sure she would beat cancer. I was with her through her first chemotherapy treatments, her mastectomy, and a brutal recovery. She did it: she beat cancer.

After four years, it was back and worse than before. And what was even harder, my mother no longer had the strength to fight. In the years preceding her second diagnosis, she had lost nearly everything she owned in the aftermath of Hurricane Katrina. Her house, her car, irreplaceable photos, and all the material things she held dear were gone. Loss and despair beat her down. When her cancer returned with a vengeance, it was nearly too much to bear. Oh, she fought but not with the same strength and positive outlook as before.

Her body betrayed her too. The food she loved no longer tasted good. It became difficult to hold a phone to her ear. Her fluid-filled legs couldn't support her. She could no longer walk, though she tried, and it took two of us to lift her crumpled body off the floor.

When she wasn't being rushed to the hospital, she spent days that turned into months in a hospital bed near a window in her bedroom. There was no pain—just the knowledge of knowing death was near. Even when she couldn't do for herself, she didn't want me or my sister to help her. While we wanted to spend as much time with her as we could, even if it meant tending to her every need, she couldn't bear the thought of being a burden to her kids.

I asked her oncologist if there was anything he could do to make her better. He said he could keep her alive, but she would be no better than she is today. No better meant she wouldn't be able to walk, and she would live confined to a bed, essentially alive but not living at all. The nurses we hired would be at her bedside twenty-four hours a day. She made it clear that she couldn't live that way. I had to admit I wouldn't want her to live that way either. The tears wouldn't stop.

The day she died was the hardest day of my life. When she left this earth, she took part of my soul with her.

I always believed that I could truly do anything or be anything if my mother was by my side. The world was limitless until that day.

The soul-crushing grief was overwhelming. It was many years before its grip loosened and I could start the journey of healing. I realized then when the hurt is so deep and all consuming, you just need to breathe and know that you are doing the best you can. You can get through it and you will get through it.

On my hardest, darkest days, I still lean on my mother's courage. Georgia Mitchell is still the strongest woman I know. Even as I tell her story, the tears are falling. I know she's not physically here, but I carry her with me every day.

CHAPTER 14

YOU ARE ENOUGH

—

I need to see my own beauty and to continue to be reminded that I am enough, that I am worthy of love without effort, that I am beautiful, that the texture of my hair and the shape of my curves, the size of my lips, the color of my skin, and the feelings that I have are all worthy and okay.

—TRACEE ELLIS ROSS

This is the best time ever to figure out your life and discover your purpose. Every one of us has unique gifts. We were put on this earth for a reason. Our lives have meaning. You're never too old or too anything to try. Just turn down the volume of your self-doubt and know you are enough.

It is what divorce coach Cherie Morris repeats every day as she meditates. Her mantra: I am enough. It is enough. She says just being is enough. "Whenever someone says to me you can't, you shouldn't, you didn't, I remind myself that whatever it is I have done, I am enough. Fundamentally, whatever I have done, it is enough."

The power of her words dominated our conversation which flowed effortlessly through the details of her divorce, the death of her parents, and the power of standing strong.

For Cherie, divorce was not just the end of her marriage. She and her former husband had their own law firm. They had to part ways from the firm too. Her life took a real pivot, but she did have help, a good lawyer, a good finance person, and a good therapist. What she didn't have was someone to help her navigate the minefield of coparenting and communicating with her ex. She explains, "What I did was choose a pivot point and really, from my perspective, try to make the best of what was a very difficult circumstance for me and my kids. And I hope in some small measure what I give back to my clients is meaningful to them. It's certainly been a journey."

The journey wasn't without bumps and bruises. Her youngest daughter went through a mental health crisis. Cherie's elderly parents were at varying stages of death and dying. She's an only child and had to take care of her parents, her four children, and, most importantly, herself. Sitting in place wasn't an option, Cherie says. "I had people to take care of and money to earn. I needed to look forward. I'm a strong feminist. I wasn't ever going to let somebody think that my soon-to-be ex-husband was going to thrive more than I would. It was very important for me to model to my daughters this is how a woman copes with adversity. Stand up strong."

Cherie learned to let go of the past hurt and pain and continues to move forward. That's not always easy to do. Past pain can be paralyzing, making it impossible to move on. But what if you can find the lesson in the pain and trauma and learn to let them go? It's possible.

As a reminder to herself and her clients, Cherie keeps a lighted whiteboard in her office. According to her, it says "Can you let it go?" She believes, "In a way, it's the work for all of us in this space of transformation because for so many of my clients, so much of their time has been reliving what has occurred and reasons for not shifting their perspective. When we start to recognize that holding on to it is not supportive for us, everything changes. It continues to be my work also."

Cherie's practice as a divorce coach and parent coordinator is thriving. She finds joy and purpose in bringing people together to find commonalities instead of their differences. Cherie says, "I'm full of the space of holding people's whatever it is, their hurt, their pain, their practical question, and their communication issues." She adds, "When I can feel productive and empathetic in the work I'm doing for other people, it gives back to me more than I've ever given to anyone."

Give yourself permission to be your extraordinary self. Know that where you are or who you are is enough.

Unfortunately, Tara Gorman didn't always get that kind of encouragement as a young child. She often heard she is "not enough" or it's "not possible."

Tara is a mom, a widow, an attorney, a producer, a professor, a philanthropist, and pretty much anything she wants to be. She's learned to live life on her terms thanks to a beloved aunt who told her she could do whatever she wanted to do. And she did.

In high school, if there wasn't a club for something she was interested in, Tara created one. When she was told she couldn't be a pom-pom girl and be in the school play since their rehearsals were at the same time, she said, "No problem." These activities were two floors apart. So, she ran down to pom practice when the rehearsal wasn't her scene and ran back in time for her scene. "No" wasn't an option for Tara.

Tara is amazingly focused and driven. When she talks about what she has done, what she plans to do, what's happened to her and for her, the moments in her life ran like scenes from a movie. Her life story drew me in and became more vivid as the details flowed. She has run a triathlon, started a fitness company, created a sexy widow's club, and clerked for a judge. She also started a production company with friends. They've already turned out an award-winning movie about an athlete who discovers how far she can push her mind and body. I thought to myself, "My God, how does this woman do it?" So, I asked her.

Tara answered, "I'm going to listen to my own inside voice. It says, 'Sure, why not? Let's try it.'"

Simply trying is the first step. That dream you've been dreaming. Put it into action. The plan you've gone over in your head time and time again? Make it happen. It doesn't matter if someone has done it before. They haven't done it quite like you. Stop with the excuses and, as Tara would say, "Let's try it."

Tara is dyslexic, but that didn't stop her from getting her MBA. She managed to push fear and self-doubt aside and not let what others may call a disadvantage hold her back. One degree wasn't enough. She wanted more, saying, "Wouldn't that shock everybody if this aerobics instructor who is dyslexic got an MBA/JD? That was a pinnacle moment in my life."

Self-doubt is a battle even for Tara from time to time. It crept in when she was in school, convincing her she was too old to be graduating in her late thirties. A cousin gave her the push she needed to unleash her negative thoughts. She told Tara, "You're going to be thirty-eight anyway. You're going to be thirty-eight with a law degree or thirty-eight without a law degree." Simple and brilliant!

Tara didn't just get her MBA/JD; she excelled. She scored in the top 3 percent on the LSAT and got her business and law degrees at the same time from two different universities. She did her MBA first at the University of Maryland and finished in the middle of her second year of law school at Georgetown University.

"So, I was on the path to be a lawyer and a judicial clerkship became available. I was told I couldn't apply. But I thought, 'Oh my God, just try.'"

Tara decided to stand out by packing her application in a purple folder. The judge's secretary saw that it was different, set it aside, and later hired her.

Tara follows the path of her inner voice so well that you may think life has dealt her an easy hand. But if you riffle through her hand, you'll see that it's far from a grand slam.

Anyone else may have fallen under the blows life dealt her.

Tara met her husband, Michael, when they were in a rock and roll band together. He was a cabinet maker and a musician. They got married after her first year of law school. When their first child was just a baby, they found out Child Protective Services was planning to take custody of their three nephews who lived in Florida. Their dad, her husband's brother, was in jail. The mom, who was on drugs, agreed to give Tara and Michael temporary custody so she could go to rehab. That was spring of 2004.

Tara, a new attorney and new mom, was working outside the house. Michael was a stay-at-home dad. With four boys in the house, Michael and Tara decided to have another child, a little girl. Just a few years after she was born, Michael got really sick and passed away. Grieving and lost, Tara did what she always does—just try.

Not really knowing how to parent her five children, Tara signed up for a parenting class. She had to work, do the laundry, mow the lawn, and do all the other thankless jobs that come with being a single mother. This meant she didn't have the extra time she needed to get all the children to all their extracurricular activities.

"There's a lot of guilt from society about if something doesn't benefit your kids, then you shouldn't be doing it," says Tara. "And I don't subscribe to that."

Instead of running around following the children, Tara decided they would follow her. When she was producing movies, she found them fun and exciting jobs on the set.

"I brought all five kids of mine to work on the movie. Matt, who was at a time where he was not in school, worked full time as a production assistant. The other three all worked as production assistants when they could. And it was great! Tinley was nine years old and the right-hand person to the assistant directors, the one who says, 'Cut, rolling.'"

Tara is still doing the lawyer thing and working on a few films at her production company. Starting the sexy widow's club was a silly, fun, and important part of her grieving Michael's passing. She plans regular music parties to keep music in the house. She is driven by her inner calling and always pushing forward.

When you are dealt a hard blow, continue to believe in yourself. Don't take yourself for granted. Turn down the volume of other people's noise and your own self-doubt, and make the decision to trust yourself. Remember, you are enough. It is enough.

CONCLUSION

Even if it makes others uncomfortable,
I will love who I am.

—JANELLE MONÁE

There's no turning back. You're here now. You have been sitting in place for far too long. It's time to stir the pot, push limits, and kick up some drama, in a good way. We need to find out what's cooking in your pot.

I'm giving you permission to light the torch. Set fire to criticism and self-doubt. Scorch your past woes and set ablaze your future. Don't let someone else tell you who you are. Get a sense of your own power.

Whatever trauma or trouble you've been through, it's over. Learn the lesson and say, "Whew, I'm not going to do that again." Move on. Our problems are never as big as we think they are. When you're going through it, you think you are the only one who has ever had it this bad. Wrong! I promise someone has had it worse than you. Remember, we walk no journey alone. There is help out there, and there are people to lean on. Surround yourself with those people, the ones who love you and want you to succeed.

Here you stand. So, hold your head a little higher, pull back your shoulders, and know that your life has meaning. Stop trying to please others. Who cares what they think? Their expectations of you simply don't matter. Stop comparing. You don't need to be perfect.

Wake up every day giddy, excited to find out what amazing thing is going to happen next. You know you are meant to do something bigger than what you're doing right now. I truly believe that we are all here on this earth for a reason. My reason is very different from your reason, but we all have a reason. We all have gifts that we can offer, right? We all have a purpose. You need to get on that path—the path of finding meaning and getting unstuck.

When you have a purpose in life, you can deny that purpose to your own peril. Be obedient to your calling.

The difference between you and Oprah and the other women you've met in this book is that they know why they're here and they see life as one big, incredible adventure. They know they're doing exactly what they believe they are here to do. As they continue on their unique journey, they find more and more success and joy.

I hope you felt your own spark as you read the soul-stirring stories of these women. I hope they inspired you to say, "Oh my God, I can do that"—whatever "that" is for you—or inspired you to change your narrative. Instead of saying, "I can't," you will say, "I will," and know that you truly can do that big thing because there are so many other women out there actually doing it. Let them be your inspiration to recognize the meaning and value of your own life and the future right in front of you.

By changing the way you see the world, the way you think, you will change your life. Believe in things that are not right in front of you. Explore. Step out of your comfort zone.

Walk into tomorrow putting yourself first. There is only one you! No one else has your gifts or talents. Start living your life on purpose. Just take the first step. You may stumble or fall flat on your face. Know that failing has nothing to do with you being a failure. It's just another life lesson.

I don't pretend to know it all. I don't! But I do know that every day is a gift. I wake up every day living my life on purpose, accepting what I already have, and sharing it with others. I know that the things I have done I didn't do on my own. None of us do much of anything on our own. Sometimes we have to lean on the shoulders of others who are strong enough to hold us up.

Luck or the universe aren't always on our side. Bad things do happen. I grieve. I might cuss. But after I get out of the fury, I can see the experience as a lesson. I learn and move on saying, "Whew! Don't do that again."

What I know for sure is that you find your purpose when you accept what is given, when you own your magic. Your purpose is ever evolving and encompasses every aspect of your life. You may find purpose in the work you do, the life you live, or the time you give.

One of my many gifts is storytelling. Whether it's reporting the big news of the day, retelling someone's story, or just sharing details of my own life, I love a good story. We're all creating stories. You are the author of your own life. So, what are you going to write? What do you want your story to be? And when are you going to start living it? My hope is that when your book of life is finished, you will look back through the pages and say it was a wild and wonderful ride, full of meaning and purpose.

Take a big leap and start writing the book of life you will be proud of. Commit to believing in yourself. Trust yourself and become that person you were meant to be. Believe in your own dreams and trust that you are enough.

Saying "no" can be a good thing. Start setting boundaries. Love yourself. Love all your flaws and rough edges, the curves and the scars. You can't truly love others until you are able to love and accept yourself.

Actor and comedian Tiffany Haddish talked to my author circle. As you can imagine, she was a riot but also open and honest. She talked about being homeless. She couldn't read but got by memorizing and mimicking. People told her she was stupid, but she had a desire to learn. Tiffany believes if you're weak in one area, you have a superpower in another. She dropped her wisdom of what she would have told her twenty-one-year-old self:

- Stop hiding. Stop pretending to be something you're not.

- Stop trying to fit in with people who don't even know your last name.

- Look in the mirror. Love and approve yourself. Then everyone else will, too.

- How you treat yourself is how the world will treat you.

Believe with every ounce of your being that you deserve to be happy. You deserve to be loved. You deserve to step into your purpose. When you begin to follow your calling, the possibilities are endless. Unleash your superpower so we can all witness the phenomenal, authentic you.

There is no road map because we are each on our own journeys.

While on my own path, I decided to dig a little deeper into my spiritual journey. I took a quick five-day trip to Canyon Ranch, a holistic wellness resort and spa in Tucson, Arizona. Away from the busyness of a metropolitan city, I found peace and serenity. I was able to conquer my fear of the unknown and did things I thought I would never do.

I learned to mediate, finally clearing the noise, and could hear my own thoughts and inner voice. I climbed a mountain and, three hours later, I made it back down to base smelling like a bear but feeling an insane rush of accomplishment.

I nervously tried acupuncture for the first time. It was amazing! I remember as I laid there with needles stuck in various points of my body from head to toe, I thought there must be drugs on the tips of these needles. I felt so good, as if I was floating. I didn't have a worry in the world. When I mentioned it to the therapist, she just laughed and said that's your qi. I now have acupuncture every two weeks to help with balance and flow.

One of the best things I did while at Canyon Ranch was meet with an astrologer, Will. Will helped me identify my gifts and get a sense of my own power. He told me to have faith and stop wasting time getting caught up in the details. I learned that people come to me every day with a message. I should use their messages as a road map on my spiritual journey. He suggested that I follow my curiosity over the next ten years. My biggest takeaways: I have a voice and a message that people are willing to listen to. Get a sense of your own power, and help others find theirs.

That was back in the fall of 2019. I was a skeptic and had never been to an astrologer before. I wasn't sure if Will said this to everyone. He had recorded our conversation and gave me a thumb drive of the recording. As I was writing this book, I needed inspiration. So, I pulled out the thumb drive and listened to it. I got goosebumps. Will had predicted that I would write a book and publish in the fall of 2021. Crazy! Now, I'll be honest, I didn't remember that part of our conversation. I'm not sure if it was tucked away somewhere in the back corners of my mind or if the stars were really aligned. I believe they were. He went on to say, "Recognize your gifts and step into them. It's not about you. It's about the mission."

I leave you with those same words: recognize your gifts, and step into them.

Every moment is a miracle, and every woman is magnificent. It's not always about you. It's about the mission. You have gifts. Start using them. Step into your calling.

Start stirring the pot, and remember you are enough.

You inspire me! I hear you. I see you.

Now, go and disrupt the universe.

APPENDIX

INTRODUCTION
Hill, Patrick L., and Nicholas A. Turiano. "Purpose in Life as a Predictor of
Mortality Across Adulthood." *Psychological Science* 25, no. 7 (July 2014): 1482–86.
https://doi.org/10.1177/0956797614531799.

CHAPTER 1
Vera, Amir. "Here are the Top Moments from the Class of 2020's Graduation Night."
CNN, May 16, 2020.
https://www.cnn.com/2020/05/17/us/graduation-2020-roundup/index.html.

CHAPTER 2
PBS. "In Performance at the White House: Women of Soul." April 6, 2014. Video, 55:57.
https://www.youtube.com/watch?v=1NwMyoLfCuQ.

TED. "Caroline McHugh: The art of being yourself." December 29, 2016. Video, 12:30.
https://www.youtube.com/watch?v=g5H5u6Eg4fM.

CHAPTER 11
Kaufman, Scott Barry. "Hansgrohe Study: The Brightest Ideas Begin In the Shower."
Plumbing & Mechanical, January 26, 2015.
www.pmmag.com/articles/96968-hansgrohe-study-the-brightest-ideas-begin-in-
the-shower.

Reddit. Shower Thoughts. "When You're a Kid, You Don't Realize You're Also Watching
Your Mom and Dad Grow Up." Thread Comment. 2019.
https://www.reddit.com/r/Showerthoughts/comments/awd1ou/when_youre_a_kid_
you_dont_realize_youre_also/ref=share&ref_source=embed&utm_content=title&utm_
medium=post_embed&utm_name=f8501adee6914b3b8eaad90c6bea66b0&utm_
source=embedly&utm_term=awd1ou.

Reddit. Shower Thoughts. "Night before a Day off Is More Satisfying Than the Actual Day Off." Thread Comment. 2019.
https://www.reddit.com/r/Showerthoughts/comments/c79pyg/night_before_a_day_off_is_more_satisfying_than/ref=share&ref_source=embed&utm_content=title&utm_medium=post_embed&utm_name=030d231e20a54075ba08a30e6bea3c63&utm_source=embedly&utm_term=c79pyg.

Reddit. Shower Thoughts. "Biting Your Tongue While Eating Is a Perfect Example of How you Can Still Screw Up, Even with Decades of Experience." Thread Comment. 2020.
https://www.reddit.com/r/Showerthoughts/comments/d8dogc/biting_your_tongue_while_eating_is_a_perfect/ref=share&ref_source=embed&utm_content=body&utm_medium=post_embed&utm_name=6cedde4809e6439faba2b193c2513588&utm_source=embedly&utm_term=d8dogc.

Reddit. Shower Thoughts. "Growing Up is Realizing You Get More Joy Out of Seeing Others Open Presents Than You Do From Opening your Own." Thread Comment. 2020
https://www.reddit.com/r/Showerthoughts/comments/efk94f/growing_up_is_realizing_you_get_more_joy_out_of/ref=share&ref_source=embed&utm_content=title&utm_medium=post_embed&utm_name=24abe56bfe9b48f789f1fd31039a0d83&utm_source=embedly&utm_term=efk94f.

Skin Cancer Foundation. "Mohs Surgery—The Most Effective Technique for Treating Common Skin Cancers." *Treatment Resources*. Accessed June 30, 2020. www.skincancer.org/treatment-resources/mohs-surgery/.

CHAPTER 12

Palmiter, David, Mary Alvord, Lillian Comas-Diaz, Suniya S. Luthar, and Salvatore R. Maddi, Katherine O'Neill, Karen W. Saakvitne, and Richard Glenn Tedeschi. "Building Your Resilience." 2012.
https://www.apa.org/topics/resilience.